BRANCH RICKEY'S
LITTLE BLUE BOOK

BRANCH RICKEY'S
LITTLE BLUE BOOK

Wit and Strategy From Baseball's
Last Wise Man

Preface by
Stan Musial

Edited from private papers and public writings by
JOHN J. MONTELEONE

A MOUNTAIN LION BOOK
MACMILLAN ♦ USA

MACMILLAN
A Simon & Schuster Macmillan Company
15 Columbus Circle
New York, NY 10023

Copyright ©1995 by Mountain Lion, Inc. Illustrations ©1995 Mountain Lion, Inc., Bob Carroll. Book design by Jon Romer and Trejo Production.

MACMILLAN is a registered trademark of Macmillan, Inc.

Rickey, Branch, 1881–1965.
    Branch Rickey's little blue book : wit and strategy from
baseball's last wise man / introduction by Stan Musial ; edited from
private papers and public writings by John J. Monteleone.
        p.   cm.
    "A Mountain Lion book."
    ISBN 0-02-860400-8
      1. Rickey, Branch, 1881–1965—Miscellanea. 2. Baseball—United
States—History—Miscellanea.   I. Monteleone, John J. II. Title.
    GV867.3.R53 1995
    796.357'02—dc20   95-4146
                                                    CIP

Manufactured in the United States of America

10 9 8 7 6 5 4 3 2 1

CONTENTS

BRANCH RICKEY'S
LITTLE BLUE BOOK

Preface

I'm glad that Branch Rickey decided he liked baseball as a profession, rather than religion, politics or the law. He was an evangelistic spell-binder and very smart.

As you'll read, Mr. Rickey—almost everyone called him "Mister"—was a many-splendored man. Even before I ever met Mr. Rickey, I'd heard and read a lot about him. He was important in my unbelievably fast climb from dead-armed Class "D" pitcher to major-league hitter within one year. At the time of his death, in late 1964, we were reasonably close. I was vice-president of the Cardinals, and he had been senior consultant to [Cardinal owner] Gussie Busch.

Rickey was still inspirational at 84, when, in the final months of his life, he was inducted into the Missouri Sports Hall of Fame. By then, Rickey had been dismissed by Busch because Rickey had gone too far in usurping the authority of the Cardinals' successful general manager, Bing Devine.

Yes, Rickey made mistakes. He was referred to as "B.R.," as "Mahatma" in New York (pretty apt), and cruelly as, "El Cheapo." The man's warts show in this book because, the fact is, all of us are human. Happily, Rickey's plusses far outweigh the minuses.

Wesley Branch Rickey was a moral man. He would have made an impressive fire-and-brimstone preacher, an effective politician, or a tough-to-beat lawyer, whether prosecuting or defending. But this man, like many of us, was fascinated by a boy's game—baseball.

Branch Rickey did everything with youthful zest. I met him early in 1941, during my fourth professional year. It was a pivotal season. I'd come to camp with my pitching arm still weak from a late-season injury the year before. But, when I hit a long home run during a squad game, Rickey heard about it and stepped off the distance. He had me hit, then reassigned me as an outfielder to a camp in the lower minor leagues. At Albany, Georgia, in the camp-breaking player distribution, Rickey found a minor-league manager—Ollie Vanek—who would take me. Vanek had scouted me out of high school in 1937.

Vanek's ball club at Springfield, Missouri, Class "D" was the springboard to batting success for me, and Rickey gave me what we would have called, in school days, a double promotion. Every time he saw me play, I hit well, if not as hard as I did later. So, at mid-season he boosted me to Rochester, New York, just one step below the majors. When Rochester was eliminated by Newark in the playoffs, Rickey called me up to the Cardinals, then a crippled ball club hanging tough with Brooklyn in a tight pennant race. Manager Billy Southworth needed a left-handed hitter. I got my chance, and, as the saying goes, the rest is history.

In that first go-round, Rickey didn't have time to pep-talk me. However, he did sign me to a $400-a-month contract and wished me well. He always called me "Stanley." The following spring, I was the lemon of the "Grapefruit League." I had one last big preseason weekend against the old St. Louis Browns, at Sportsman's Park. Then Rickey called me in and, to my surprise, gave me a new contract at $750 a month!

Fortunately, I didn't play long enough for Rickey to have to listen to his persuasive tales at contract time (you'll read plenty about that in this book); but I wish this generously talented man had stayed with the Cardinals. His boss, Sam Breadon—with whom, for 25 years, Rickey had an Odd Couple relationship—tried unsuccessfully to wheel and deal a la Rickey. But over the next few years, the sale of players the caliber of Johnny Mize, Walker Cooper, and Murry Dickson kept the Cardinals from having a real dynasty.

We didn't have as many pennant-winning teams as we might have had, largely because Branch Rickey went to Brooklyn, where he waved the magic wand that had previously turned the St. Louis Redbirds from rags to riches while, in the process, making Mr. Rickey a lot of money. Rickey teams won eight pennants and three World

Series titles between 1926 and 1949, a record that helped him become a Hall of Famer.

Rickey sold the surplus talent he had developed. The year I came up—1941—the Cardinals' farm teams won in the toughest minor leagues—Sacramento (California), Rochester (New York), Columbus (Ohio), and Houston (Texas). After we went down to the last day to rally past Brooklyn, with 106 victories, the St. Louis Swifties handed the Yankees an upset defeat. As ballplayer-turned-broadcaster Bud Blattner put it, an all-star team of our top farm clubs probably could have finished third behind the Cardinals and Dodgers. In many ways, this was Branch Rickey's masterpiece. Not, certainly, the achievement for which he is best remembered: giving black players their long-overdue chance. As one who played with a black teammate on a western Pennsylvania playoff team in high-school basketball, I'd never felt comfortable with Jim Crow in the league.

Fortunately, our Cardinals team was managed by Eddie Dyer, a man who had tremendous respect for Jackie Robinson. Dyer made sure that we gave Robinson more deference than any team in the league. Personally, I had mixed emotions about Robinson. On one hand I was glad to see the color barrier smashed, but when Jackie edged out Enos Slaughter and me for the 1949 batting title, I knew the Dodgers were now the team to beat in the National League. In fact, the Cardinals never won a pennant while Robinson was an active player. I can also thank Mr. Rickey for making it possible for me to have teammates like Curt Flood and Bill White, two men whose contributions to baseball stretched far beyond the diamond. You know, Willie Mays always said that when he looks at his wallet he thinks of Jackie Robinson. Well, he should think of Rickey too!

When Branch Rickey rubbed out the reprehensible color line in baseball, it reminded me of one of his more colorful lines: "An addition by subtraction."

—Stan Musial

Introduction

I learned about the collection of Mr. Rickey's personal papers through a chance meeting with David Berman, a librarian assistant who had worked for awhile at the Library of Congress' manuscript division. And when David shared some of Mr. Rickey's player scouting reports he had read, I was hooked.

However, when I arrived at the Library of Congress, I was not prepared for the voluminous amount of material on file—131 containers of Mr. Rickey's writings, correspondence, and speeches. Material pertaining to the failed Continental League alone occupied seven containers. In fact, Mr. Rickey not only was a great "sayer," but also a great saver. Included among the treasures were employment contracts, award certificates, and receipts (along with fabric swatches) from his personal tailor. But the treasure boxes were also full of what I'd hoped for: scores of scouting reports on every conceivable level of players, from future hall of famers to anonymous bushers; hundreds of lectures on how to play, how to scout and judge talent, and more; scores of speeches on pressing political and social issues of the day; dozens of comments on character traits that yield success and many memos, notes and articles on the legal, administrative, and business issues of baseball. Who wouldn't be intrigued by an article, "Why Toronto Belongs in Major League Baseball," written more than three decades ago?

When reading Mr. Rickey's private papers and letters, such as his always optimistic missives to Bing Crosby, part owner of the Pittsburgh Pirates, or his "three abides," a treatise delivered at dinner to his daughters on the requisite traits of a suitable suitor, I felt a sense of good fortune to have discovered so many wise and intelligent thoughts not only on the game of baseball but on life itself. He had a wide range of interests. As a young man he was a rural school teacher, a lay preacher and once was considered as a nominee for governor of Missouri. His writings revealed a man of tremendous intellect and indomitable drive. He seemed torn by unresolvable conflict. He

appeared to be the man of ultimate paradoxes, a capitalist/moralist/
competitor/do-gooder/visionary/reactionary all rolled into one.

For such a complicated individual as Mr. Rickey, what better way
to reveal his mercurial nature than to present a sampling of his own
words, on varied subjects from baserunning to religion, with his often
astute and witty scouting reports sprinkled throughout the text. The
book ends with the comments of his contemporaries—the players,
scouts, managers and sportswriters. As Mr. Rickey judged, so he was
judged.

With judicious consideration of this selection of Rickeyisms and
others' reflections, each reader can come to his or her own true understanding and assessment of the man. And in the end, this little book,
as intended, will go a long way toward revealing the heart, soul, and
mind of baseball's last wise man.

—John J. Monteleone

Epigraph

To say that Branch Rickey was the finest man ever brought to the game of baseball is to damn with the faintest praise—like describing Stern as a lively fiddler. From the day in 1903, when Rickey signed on as a catcher for the LeMars, Iowa, team, at $150 a month, he was a giant among pygmies. If his goal had been the United States Supreme Court instead of the Cincinnati Reds, he would have been a giant on the bench.

—Red Smith

CHAPTER ONE

Character Matters

To Rickey, character was the key. No matter what a man's pursuit, if he was an honest man and treated others fairly, and gave his best efforts, then he was on the road to success. This chapter is devoted to Rickey's ideas on potential, character, and winning.

On Effort and Excellence

They go to work consumed with a burning purpose to accomplish a definite something, and they willingly pay the price for that something. These are the chaps who become educated in my game.

A man who isn't alert is usually in the second division, and that's where he belongs.

Don't shift too much responsibility for your success in this game to somebody else. You rely pretty much on yourself. Be anxious about it. Be persevering about it. Be firm about it. Have a high purpose. Pay the price. Pay whatever it takes, and you'll come out where merit takes you.

Sweat is the greatest solvent there is for most players' problems. I know of no cure, no soluble way to get rid of a bad technique as quick as "sweat." The same thing is true on the part of the coach or teacher—infinite patience. Make a man do it over and over again. Right there with patience are industry and constant work on the thing. If you just accomplish one little thing, you may move a man from the minor leagues to the majors.

It's so hard for all of us to do things we don't do well. It's so hard for a man voluntarily to repeat a task where he has no artistry. He feels defeated all the time because he can't do it well. At the end of every effort, it says "quit"—do something else that you can do more gracefully. The fellow finally succumbs to that, and he gives up or turns away, or he doesn't take the time he should to complete his assignment. I see pitchers who are told to throw 25 balls today, 25 tomorrow and the next day. Some will do it, but others will throw eight or ten and then quit. I know about this. I've done it myself.

Spring training lecture: We have 140 men here, and there will be about 35 more in the next few days, making about 175 men altogether. One man comes in one minute late, which takes the time of at least 150 men, and that is 150 minutes, which would make him two and a half hours late. There will be men late, and sometimes unavoidably so. Rather than stay outside, they come in ten minutes late, if necessary. That's 1,500 minutes, or 250 hours. On the field, when you're called, don't just walk over; come double-time, get there fast. Men are waiting until you do. I want you (managers and coaches) to assume responsibility—send the players out of this camp better boys, so that if they fail in baseball they can get a recommendation to be a coach or director of physical education.

It is amazing to me that men who want to be excellent—meaning they want to excel in what they do—and select baseball as their profession, their livelihood, make their money out of it, build their home out of it, make baseball their primary earning agency—and then they will be content to drone through all the years with plausible, noticeable, correctable faults. I don't understand that kind of energy. I don't care if I was a ditch-digger at $1 a day and paying my own board, I'd want to do my job better than the fellow next to me. I'd want to be the best at whatever I do.

President Abraham Lincoln sat in his chair almost all the time, and there was no more industrious man than he. Industry is not the expenditure of shoe leather. It is having ideas—ideas about the job you hold, how to improve it and yourself.

I don't understand a man who won't practice, who is satisfied, perfectly happy to be mediocre—when he might be great. He goes to his grave with the label on his coffin: dumb. But he wasn't dumb; he just had no great energy, no great purpose. He was satisfied to be mediocre. It's too bad, whether it's a student in college or in a man's business; it's just too bad.

As great as Ty Cobb was, if he saw anybody doing anything, no matter what it was, he wanted to do it better. Dizzy Dean had it. Never saw a man throwing a ball that he didn't have an uncontrollable yen to do it, and beat him at it, before the sun went down the next day. If you want to be as great as Cobb or Dean, you must impose on yourself tasks you don't like. You only broad jump eight feet, but you have to go nine to compete and make a living. You better go practice, whether you like it or not.

◇

A winner gets completely saturated with the desire to excel. He is on the high road to a personal championship. It makes men willing—indeed, anxious—to devote themselves with perhaps exclusive attention to their weaknesses. This consuming desire can make a faulty, youthful batsman like Enos Slaughter into a great batsman. It can make a good baserunner out of a slow runner. The greatest single thing that makes a championship player is his desire to be one. The greatest single quality of a championship club is a collective, dominating urge to win.

◇

Wanting to do something—desire—is the greatest difference between a championship team and a team in the second division.

◇

I heard a manager say: "Well, if he didn't have that particular pitch, he would not even be in professional ball, and here he is, going in the majors or he's in AAA." Well, it's just as sensible to say that if Paderewski couldn't play a piano, he'd starve to death. The thing Paderewski's doing is the thing he's practiced since he was eight years of age, for approximately eight hours a day in the first twenty years of his life, solemnly sitting at a piano preparing to do this particular thing. The mark of distinction that the man reaches is earned; it isn't an accident. You can't say that, if he couldn't do this thing, he would be no good. The fact is—he's paid a tremendous price to be able to do this particular little thing.

> **PROSPECTS AND SUSPECTS Richard Groat** ♦ This boy will graduate from Duke this coming June (1951). He is a fair runner, very good arm, and good batting form. The best thing about Groat is his dispostion, his desire to play and to win. He has unusually good coordination and could play shortstop on the Pittsburgh club much better than anyone we now have. It would not even be necessary to send him to any minor league club. *Richard ("Dick") Groat played 14+ seasons in the major leagues. He was the National League Most Valuable Player in 1960, and played on World Series winners in Pittsburgh (1960) and St. Louis (1964).*

With three hundred players in one professional baseball camp at Vero Beach (the Brooklyn Dodgers' training camp), I did not need the imposition of any disciplinary rule when I had every one of the 300 physically tired at dusk.

If things come easy, there is no premium on effort. That's the great, deep fault of the signing "bonus" in my business. There should be joy in the chase, zest in the pursuit.

If building character is part of a college education, then you should put the boy in professional athletics and keep him honest rather than professionalize him, as in reality you do, on your own [college] team. Having a degree doesn't mean anything. It's the man who finds interest and zest in his work that counts. It isn't catching the fox; it's running him down that is the interest. It's in having your ability approach your capacity.

Embrace Everything: Adventure and Discipline

Think a lot, and don't throw away your time. Embrace everything that will be of benefit to you.

Men who do only what they want to do can become very narrow.

Frankly, I would prefer a player who will embrace rational adventure than a field full of know-it-alls who do nothing. Anatole France said it better. Speaking to the French Assembly at a time of great stress in his country, he said: "I prefer the errors of enthusiasm to the indifference of wisdom."

There are two kinds of players—players that do not respond well to bad plays, and those that respond definitely. The first man strikes out. He knows that the last pitch was a bad ball, and he didn't mean to swing. Now he is mad that he did. But the catcher misses the ball, and the hitter can't recover quick enough to get started to first base before the ball. This man doesn't recover quick enough from despondency to overcome it. But the champion doesn't let the play affect him this way. If this man strikes out, he'll show he isn't happy about it; but he controls his temper and keeps his poise. That's the difference between a winner and a loser. The winner can meet the next challenge.

We must do our level best to get men in the frame of mind to elect to impose their own restrictions. Discipline should come from within. It's more effective. When you have discipline as a result of compulsion; when you have discipline of an individual as a result of outside pressure; when it comes following a sense of fear, if the fear of penalty or if the fact of penalty is the thing that makes the man correct—then he's a dangerous man.

Proper discipline is elective. You choose to do it. The arrival of the correct discipline of an individual is an educative process. It comes by way of a man recognizing—gradually and perhaps fully—finally, and embracing a theory, a practice, a principle, a fundamental attitude toward life and life itself.

Basic honesty allows a man to go to the mirror, look himself in the face, and not be ashamed ever.

Men have a tendency to think the thing they're not doing is more inviting than the thing they are doing. And men don't get many satisfactions out of the thing they are doing.

There's a cause, there's an effect. The law of it in your lives—in everything you do—is just as inexorable as the law of cause and effect. You think a certain way, and it's just as sure to bring a characteristic, a definite response to your thinking, as it would if you hit a drumstick on a drumhead and made a noise.

You boys know me—I have a personal background that has sort of put me on a pedestal: he's a goody-goody fellow, he's a pin-cushion moralist, he's a softy. Well maybe so. A man can't estimate himself like other people can judge him to be in character. If there are some of the habiliments of hypocrisy that you can't remove, the best thing is not to talk about them and live your life the best you can. Do the best you can. This thing I have done was a thing that I felt I had to do. I could not do otherwise.

Some years ago, when I was managing the St. Louis Browns, I lost a game in Detroit in the last half of the eleventh inning in a very unusual manner. Detroit came to bat in a tie-score game. Two men out and nobody on the bases when a player named Ty Cobb came to bat. He got a base on balls and scored the winning run without another ball being pitched to another batsman. By sheer adventure and skill, he caused two errors. There were four breaks in his favor, all caused only by himself. His daring at first, his boldness and skillful turn at second, his characteristic slide ten feet before he reached third, his quick mind and quick body following his slide. All four contrived to send him home and really made a home run out of a base on balls. In the very same game there was a player on my team by the name of Jim, I will call him. He was in the majors three of four years. He was a fine physical specimen. He and Cobb were about the same age—the same weight and height. Their running speed almost the same. My faulty outfielder had a stronger arm than Cobb and more driving power at the bat. The one rose to unparalleled fame, while the other lived and rests in obscurity. Cobb wanted to do something so much that nothing else mattered; and Jim punched the clock.

◊

You can, even in a trial workout of twenty minutes with a man alone under favorable conditions, get a definite and, I sometimes think, fairly reliable piece of information on a player's disposition. You can acquire an impression of the man's intelligence and aptitude, and, perhaps sometimes, little points on his personality that are decisive and dependable.

If you are mentally apt, you can turn every supposed reversal into an "All Right." What a blessing in disguise.

It is not the honor that you take with you, but the heritage you leave behind.

PROSPECTS AND SUSPECTS **Jackie Brown** ♦ He was born prematurely, and has never caught up. I don't think he ever has a thought. He has never related an incident in his life, never told a story in his life, never had a belly laugh in his life. He would be incapable of comprehension to so deep a point. He is as near animal instinct and as far away from human intelligence as a man can be and retain human form. He has all the pitches. I would be less surprised to hear him suddenly bark like a dog at nothing than I would to see him pitch a thoughtful inning. He has two arms and two legs, two eyes, and in fact, all body organs seem to function. How could mother nature cheat him so sadly upstairs? He might shut the Brooklyn club out any old day but more likely will walk the first half dozen men to face him if he ever pitches against Brooklyn. Jack has plenty of things besides baseball to worry about. He has a wife and baby living with about 15 other poor folk in a four-room house. He is a 20-game winner—major-league stuff. Just too bad he was brought up. Chiefly I am to blame for it.

Don't be idle. Idleness is the most damnable thing. And don't be idle in uniform when you're not playing.

First of all, a man, whether seeking achievement on the athletic field or in business, must want to win. He must feel the thing he is doing is worthwhile; so worthwhile that he is willing to pay the price of success to attain distinction.

PROSPECTS AND SUSPECTS **Stan Willis** ♦ Quick mind. Affable. Nice boy. Not a dummy. If he didn't make good grades in high school it would be simply because he didn't give a darn. His father and mother and grandparents on both sides were smart enough. He is the sort of fellow who is looking for new worlds to conquer. "Show me something else you want me to do," is his continuous slogan. I like him. He is worthwhile as a pitcher. He would need to be sent to a careful manager. He could become a ladies' man or a good drinker. He could go a long way in the professional game. He is worth a bonus, I wish we could sign him decently.

This is a fellow that I think everybody would like personally. If he would run for political office, he would be a tough bird to beat. He would be elected by acclamation, and it could be true that he would be qualified for any job that he himself believed he could do. *Affable Stan Willis, who answered to the nickname "Red," played 10 years, 1952–61, in the minor leagues.*

CHAPTER TWO

Luck Is the
Residue of Design

T *his chapter naturally follows the last: Rickey felt that if you applied your intelligence and labor to a task, then good fortune should visit your enterprise.*

Luck Is the Residue of Design

Things worthwhile generally just don't happen. Luck is a fact, but should not be a factor. Good luck is what is leftover after intelligence and effort have combined at their best. Negligence or indifference or inattention are usually reviewed from an unlucky seat. The law of cause and effect and causality both work the same with inexorable exactitudes. Luck is the residue of design.

Our club [the Pirates] finished in last place in 1953. We hope to find ourselves in a contending position at the earliest possible time. Therefore, we must have in mind the employment of whatever agents, or methods, or procedures, or practices or gadgets calculated to hasten the improvement of our players. No last place team, it seems to me, can rely on the play of fortune to bring to hand suddenly and without cause a coterie of great players. And it is not safe for us as directors or managers or coaches to feel that we are sufficiently resourceful and superior either in selection or observations of players that by our own super-excellence we can bring a last place club into contending position. More easily can we lift ourselves over the fence by our own boot straps.

Poverty means that you have a ball club low in the standings of the race, and it naturally follows that but very few fans turn out at the gates to see the boys play ball. If the fans fail to attend games, then your bank account is positively nil. And without money a baseball owner not only will find himself in a whale of a lot of trouble, but positively unable to raise even a finger to help rebuild his team. We have heard a great deal about economics lately, and this is the part it plays in major-league baseball. We formerly had a ball club—from 1917 to 1924, that invariably finished terribly low in the National League race. However, and let me stress this point, the Cardinals did have a few stars on the team—stars who would and did help other teams when they were sold for large sums. With the team always finishing down at the bottom of the pennant race, it was not to our advantage to sell the one or two stars on the team. The headliners were about the only incentive for the handful of fans to turn out to see a Cardinals game. Nevertheless, when you have something that the other fellow wants, you are broke, and he tantalizingly dangles a gigantic roll of folding money before your eyes, offering the sum for what you have—well, you are first tempted, and then you finally relent and sell.

On Rickey's first year with the St Louis Browns (1913): I was not accustomed to daily defeats. Michigan had been a winner. In St. Louis, though, there had been a continuous series of defeats. The Pittsburgh Pirates, the New York Giants, and the Chicago Cubs were one, two, three all the time. What could you do about it? The Browns had no money, no money even for scouts. So, through my acquaintance with college coaches, plus agreements to put out players for minor-league experience (although we couldn't always get those players back), we sought to improve and overtake the rich teams.

What better rule, when you are looking for a man to fill a job, than to apply the three questions Thomas Jefferson asked every time he made an appointment? They were: 1. Is he honest? 2. Is he capable? 3. Is he loyal to the Constitution of the United States? Substitute the more particular loyalties and devotions, like those to boss, club, and organization, instead of the one to Constitution, which we all take for granted, and you have it. Can you think of three better requisites?

You can't solve everything in a minute. Make time your ally. Delay sharp action.

A manager who is not in sole charge of his players cannot run his team, serve his employers best, and indeed, cannot call himself a manager. A few players will soon find his weakness and start managing him.

On what it takes to prosper as a first-class executive in baseball: I look first for integrity. That is a stronger word than mere honesty, and it means refusal to trim, or cut corners, or seek unfair advantage. It eliminates the fellow who may be legally honest, but who makes sharp deals. The second thing I look for is capacity for work; ability follows in the wake of fine capacity. Industry is the upshot of both.

This fellow, George Kissell, is doubtless a good manager and all that. But he is also a darn good employee. He looks after details. He is a "cleaner-upper." First man out, last man in. Impresses me as having a sense of responsibility for anything and everything; even to the insignificant things such as locating early and picking up later stray balls. I would hire him in any camp. *Rickey's report while scouting Cardinal players at Lang Field, November 8, 1962. Kissell was renamed senior field coordinator of the Cardinals in December of 1994.*

Baseball is my business, but it is much more than that. I think I still get the same thrill out of the game as I did when I was a kid. I know most of our players, their fathers, mothers, sisters, brothers, aunts, and uncles. I'm no father to them; they don't want that. I am their employer, and they have to make good; but I also want to be their friend and I will do everything I can to help them.

I do not mind public criticism. That sort of thing has not changed any program I thought was good.

I am in a business that is under scrutiny of able and facile writers continuously. I never feel more unworthy than when I think that, perhaps, unjustified criticism had something to do with changing my plans. I don't like to feel that adverse or unfair comment can or does dull the edge of my courage.

What is the purpose of a ball game? To win.

On Trading

You must know ahead of time who is failing. You must take risks.

My best trade was when I was with the Cardinals in 1931. The Cardinals didn't particularly need Hack Wilson, but I knew there was a market for him. We gave the Cubs two players for Wilson. I sold him to the Dodgers for two players whose names I can't recall and $57,000 cash. My worst deal? In 1922 I traded Cliff Heathcote to the Cubs for Max Flack late in the season. Flack came to see me with about two weeks left in the season and said he was through. I didn't figure Heathcote would make the grade, but I was fooled. Heathcote played several years for the Cubs and Flack quit as he threatened. So, in effect, I gave Heathcote away.

There are anesthetic players. You watch them all year, and you say they are not contributing much to the team. Then they show you a lot of impressive statistics. They put you to sleep with statistics that don't win games. It is time to trade a player as soon as he reaches the twilight zone of stardom.

Mr. Rickey and Giants manager John McGraw began discussions on trading St. Louis Cardinals slugger Roger Hornsby in 1919 but the trade did not go through until 1926 when infielder Frankie Frisch and pitcher Jimmy Ring were exchanged for Hornsby. Many years later, Rickey reflected on the blockbuster trade: Had I been in sole charge, Hornsby never would have left St. Louis. Depriving the Cardinals of a known quantity of greatness in batting and competitive spirit wasn't right. Whether Frisch was as good or better than Hornsby, personal affront (a roiling feud between owner Sam Breadon and Hornsby) is never enough to justify a move of such magnitude.

In trying to obtain permission from Pirate owner John Galbraith to sell slugger Ralph Kiner and then use the money to develop and buy new players, Rickey, in 1952, composed this ditty.

Babe Ruth could run. Our man cannot.

Ruth could throw. Our man cannot.

Ruth could steal a base. Our man cannot.

Ruth was a good fielder. Our man is not.

Ruth could hit with power to all fields. Our man cannot.

Ruth never requested a diminutive field to fit him. Our man does.

CHAPTER THREE

Baseball 101

*E*very aspect of baseball fascinated Rickey. He had thought through many of the finer points and here offers his views on the basics of batting, fielding, and pitching. Remember, effort plus design equals success in Rickey's game.

I know a fellow who is a shoe cobbler in my home town. Gruff sat at his cobbler's bench, and I'd sit and talk with him. He'd talk through two or three kinds of pegs in his mouth, surrounded by small hammers and other tools. He'd pay no attention seemingly to what tools he picked up and used, but the job would be done correctly. If I asked him which tool he'd used on a particular job, he wouldn't remember.

They were so much a part of him that he had used them without thinking. They might have been painted a different color, but he would have used them correctly when he needed to do a particular thing at a particular time. Just as old Gruff took years to become skillful, it may be that you will need a great length of time to have it become automatic to you, and not be confused by the mechanics of the game.

Batting was a perfect science to Tyrus Raymond Cobb. So it was with George Sisler. Read his book on the subject. It was to Tris Speaker and Eddie Collins. Both were student batsmen. I call your attention to the preparatory care and practice of approach and foot position, hand extension, and the exact bat location at the final moment when the batter presents himself to the pitch. Method and purpose command the instant coordination of almost all the muscles in his entire body to do one single little thing, namely hit an elusive round ball with a round bat. That's batting.

Hitting: Power at the Plate

There are pennants won by hitting; primarily by hitting, where the club has come to distinction because of its power—and its power was largely responsible for its getting into the World Series.

I must have subconsciously given more attention to the development of power, perhaps looked to develop run-making teams. I cotton to it and go for it. The men around me have also looked for that sort of thing. I have sometimes missed the players who are more spectacular in defensive work. My clubs have been more distinctive in run-making than in holding the opposition to a low number of runs.

PROSPECTS AND SUSPECTS **Ken Boyer** ♦ At third base, I saw the best ballplayer on first impression that I have seen in many a day. Boyer by name. He can run with very deceptive speed, and he does run. Never loafs. He has big hands, and knows what to do with them. He has a quick arm and a fine arm from his elbow on down. Every body muscle is under control. He could play shortstop and certainly would be a corking second baseman. Indeed, I think Boyer could play anywhere, and I mean anywhere. He drives the ball with great power and he is a line-drive hitter deluxe. The newspapermen down here are raving about the outfielder [Bill] Virdon, saying, in effect, unanimously that Virdon is the greatest player ever to be in Cuba, etc., etc. I will take Boyer. He must be 6′ tall and weigh 185 pounds. I was not close enough to him to risk positive accuracy on his vital statistics, but every inch of him and every pound of him is a professional player of great promise. *Ken Boyer was one of the best fielding third basemen in major-league history. He had a lifetime batting average of .287 in 15 seasons. He helped the Cardinals win the 1964 world championship.*

The home run craze largely brought about by Babe Ruth had a full part in creating an army of puny hitters trying from infancy to hit an over-the-fence trajectory—an upswing at the ball.

I have watched baseball for sixty years. I've never heard of any ballplayer adding power. I've never seen a young boy come up to the major leagues who could not hit with power and watched the coaches work with him and then seen the day come when he would hit with power. You cannot add power. You cannot add it to a batter or a runner or a pitcher or put it in the arm of an outfielder. A man is born with power. And that is it. You can correct a hitch in a batter's swing and so increase his hitting ability and bring to bear power that was being wasted, but you cannot add power. His grandparents, his great grandparents, his ancestry did or did not give him power and there isn't very much you can do about it. You can teach a man who has power to use it—and that is an art. Power is inborn, and its control and explosive use are instinctive. When you see power on the diamond it is as clear as a cannon shot. Such is the general opinion of baseball managers concerning a hitter's power. But most players do improve in batting as time goes on, and almost all players can be helped with good instruction and plenty of practice.

Runs batted in doesn't amount to a darn—maybe a little. Three things affect RBI: first, a manager who believes his team is better playing only a one-run lead, who has hitters take and take, whose team gets very little chance to hit cripples, or a manager who may have a notion that some men don't hit in runs well and waits for the next man. This affects the RBI of the man and of the team as a whole. Second, the park is a consideration. Third is the batting order; the batting order determines most.

The greatest hitter in the world will strike at bad balls occasionally because his mind is made up to hit. Don't be self-conscious, be yourself at the plate, you can do what you want to. It's not so important that you hit pitching machine balls; just that you learn to judge the strike zone by watching pitches that come into it and that will improve your hitting.

No batter will willingly embrace suggestions or change in any direction as long as he thinks his own method is correct.

Hitting: Three Basics

There are three basic things in batting—stride, hitch, and keeping the bat level.

I found out very early—and it still is true—that a man who definitely overstrides can't hit. And I know of no cure for it. I've talked to Mr. McGraw, Connie Mack, and I challenge anyone to definitely cure it.

Lots of things you can cure but overstriding is a brain lesion—it's a timing process of the mind that the man cannot judge clearly, and he steps too far. He's a home run hitter on certain pitches. But when the pitcher starts changing speeds and throwing balls that deflect from a straight line—when those combinations come upon him— he's finished. DiMaggio brings his foot up and puts it right down in the same place; Sisler strides six inches, and I don't know of any great hitters who aren't short striders.

The second thing is the hitch, which can be anything. Dropping the bat, there are a dozen ways to make a hitch, a preliminary movement that requires the batter to assume at the last possible second, some new position. The Lord knows the batter has his hands full to be ready so that the only movement after the ball is in flight is a forward movement.

Now lots of great hitters will move the bat some and it is all right that the fellow does it in time so that he becomes poised to give only a forward sweep and not drop the bat so he has to bring it up before the ball gets there. If he does, he's at a disadvantage. The hitch is bad, but it can be corrected. The correction is a forced position, as natural as you can get it, which you make him hold. Whenever you put a hitter with a hitch into a forced position, you'll see he has a tough job to keep his hands from moving. You can even take hold of the bat and tell him not to swing, and I bet when the ball goes by, you'll have a hard time to keep hold of the bat—even when he's not trying to hit.

Most of those fundamentals are easily corrected because they are habits. It is bad for a fellow to come up at the end of a swing, the big end of the bat point up, not straight around. The correction for that, as far as I know, is in batting practice that man should try to hit every ball on the ground.

There are many batters who are hurt by having information on pitches. You couldn't give a signal to a Sisler, a Cobb, and some others—they just wouldn't take it. There are some hitters that it helps immensely if they have a weakness on certain pitches. There are some men who, when they know what's coming will hit at the ball in spite of it. And there are certain types of hitters that you will make a bad-ball hitter out of by telling. But some will be helped. That's why we mention it to pitchers.

The greatest single difference between a major-league and a minor-league batsman is the difference in his judgment of the strike zone. The major leaguer knows better the difference between a ball and a strike. He knows better whether to swing or take a pitch.

If a hitter's bat goes back farther before it starts forward you can lay a coin or two out of my pocket that this batter has something simulating a hitch.

No man who starts his swing from halfway back achieves the full limit of his acceleration. This man will have no power.

You can't make hitters out of men, or give a man more power. But there's one thing you can do—help a fellow who strikes out. Mr. Manager or Coach, don't say to him, "Don't strike out." But put him on the pitching machine, that's where he'll be helped.

For example, take a righthanded hitter who strikes out a lot and have him on the pitching machine with orders to hit everything to right field. The first day he is awkward and unstable. The second day he gets three or four okay, and on the third day, the manager tells him to do it again, that he will lose some of his power but that's okay. Then you let him hit some to left, then some to right and by the fifth day, he's getting pretty disgusted with this routine and really begins to question what he is doing.

Then, Mr. Manager, you take him to your room and say, "Remember Monday, when we started, and then Tuesday, Wednesday, Thursday, and, today, Friday. I want you to go back to today's workout and Thursday's, and maybe Wednesday's and I want you to tell me how many balls you missed on those days"—and it's quite possible that he hasn't missed any—and you'll tell him to continue those exercises and you can correct his striking out.

Hitting is very much a matter of good form. Preliminary stance at the plate means nothing at all. Where his front foot may be in the preliminary position doesn't count. The hand movement, the level sweep of the bat, the length of the stride, the head movement, any of these and others can be very important when the pitch is coming. Adjustment must bring the batsman to good form at the time the ball takes flight, not before.

Another feature of batting is the direction of the sweep of the bat. The level sweep is good—variations from it correspondingly bad, and unless the batter has extraordinary power to hit the ball over the fence with his normal swing, the fly ball hitter is out of luck. The level sweep of the bat will give any batter a normal number of fly balls and ground balls. Very few good batters end their swing with the bat pointing at the sky.

On courage at bat: Courage is a by-product of form. Form is the horse and courage is the cart. Professional baseball players are not "yellow." As a class, they are not tainted with physical cowardice. I never knew one, not even a non-hitting pitcher, who was biologically "yellow." Lack of acquaintanceship with any new job produces initial indecision or hesitation or timid approach. Correct form is the forerunner to good performance, and the early cure of fear. Then courage follows.

Drills and Coaches

Coaching is a matter not of compulsion but of fertility in suggestion. It may not work for Bill like it would for Steve or John or Dick. You cannot make a law that will apply to this man's fingers, to the length of them, to the exact pressure he gives the ball, to the exact position in the hand. It won't work the same for two men. You have to be full of suggestions.

Don't take away the confidence of a man in what he now has until he agrees with you that what he has won't do. You better be on the safe side and urge him to keep what he has until what you are working on as a substitute proves better. Don't force him to abandon bad form until you have substituted good form.

A great fault of young managers is over-coaching, over-managing, over-pointing out an instinctive fault without implementing a cure. It doesn't do any good to tell a young player not to strike out. Put him in the cage and give the pitching machine high velocity and tell the batsman to hit good balls with intent. That's the cure.

Do you know that you can corrupt more hitters by interfering with them before they give up than you can ever help any living human? Don't you ever tell a pitcher how to throw before he has felt his own sense of need. I don't care if he bats crosshanded or stands on his head and pitches. Don't ever anticipate an unrealized need of a ballplayer or a man or a banker or anybody else. None of you ever get on your knees and thank God that your families are well. We may say that in a formal way in a church ritual you will thank God, but down in your hearts, you wait until Jane dies or your mother dies or something happens to you that really goes down deep. You get to the place where you can't pay your bills and you don't know what to do and you don't know where to turn and you have gone for help pretty nearly every place you could turn. Then, by George, if you have a spark of religion of any sort in you, you know where you go. You go to the source of power, to the source of authority. You go to the only place where you can get help. A coach's opportunity is a player's distress, a player's helplessness, his sense of need. That is the coach's chance. You can't anticipate it. Don't do it. Wait until he strikes out and says, "What am I doing that is wrong?"

Pitching: Poise, Control, and Stuff

In pitching we want to produce delusions, practice deceptions, make a man misjudge. We fool him—that's the whole purpose of the game. The ethics of the game of baseball would be violated if man did not practice to become proficient in deception. In other words, you can't go to heaven if you don't try to fool the batter.

I sometimes think that pitchers who put on a good show are the easiest to judge. The tricky ones are those who you dismiss out of hand. They can fool you; they can fool themselves at the outset, though not intentionally. The trouble is that there are particular pitchers who, whatever limited characteristics he has that cause you to dismiss him, can a year from now, be a different pitcher. Remember, a pitcher's repertoire of pitches is almost unlimited. There are pitchers like Dizzy Dean or, before him, Christy Mathewson, or a guy like Irv Pallica of the Brooklyn Dodgers, who have the ability to see another pitcher throw a certain pitch and go right out and duplicate it to his own benefit.

I watched Dean and Mathewson acquire screwballs and knuckle balls and then they threw them with all kinds of deflections and speeds. They acquired a knuckleball, put a change of speed on a curve ball and added masterful control of them overnight. There is no prohibition against a pitcher acquiring new pitches. They get them and forget everything else they had, and you suddenly have a new pitcher, someone you didn't even see before.

When that happens, you must praise the pitcher and be proud of him and give him credit for coming up with something that made him succeed. And you then must admit you made a mistake in your own previous judgment.

When I was a youngster and a coach at the University of Michigan (1910–12), I had no pitching. The spitball was perfectly legitimate. I put in the *Michigan Daily* an ad for anybody who could throw a ball hard to please report to the gymnasium at three o'clock on Friday afternoon. I had a raft of them and it saved the day. One or two of them came up with quite a curve ball. I gave them a spitball. The spitball was perfectly legal in that day.

The future trend of major-league clubs will see the development of relief specialists in the minors—not like the old days, when relievers were tired veteran pitchers on the way out.

Anger, frankly, is the biggest enemy a pitcher has. It is an inexcusable affliction. Anger affects the delicate workings of a great pitcher in a close ball game. No constructive thought can come out of anger. The pitcher will lose control of the ball as soon as he loses control of himself. A man who is master of himself in other ways will master himself on the mound. [Christy] Mathewson, [Grover Cleveland] Alexander, or, today, Vernon Law have never showed their feelings.

PROSPECTS AND SUSPECTS **Steve Carlton** ♦ A very tall pitcher-built boy. Long, slender, strong hands. Steve has an intelligent face, fine eyes set far apart, and intelligent conversation. He lives in Miami. His father works as a maintenance man for Pan American. A good fastball, straight as a string, but good velocity. A fair curve and decent control of it. He has a change-up on his fastball which is really a change of pace curve. This chap has the most remarkable control of this particular change-up that I have seen in a long time. He can learn to hold men on first base beyond any doubt. Good aptitude. I like this boy. I will be surprised if he doesn't go to the major leagues, perhaps sooner than later. Whoever manages him should let him alone. Don't try to over-instruct him. He simply needs to pitch. *(4/4/64) Steve Carlton spent 24 seasons in the major leagues, where he had a 329-244 record and struck out 4,136 batters. He is in the Hall of Fame.*

Carl Hubbell (New York Giants and Hall-of-Hame pitcher) produced perfect deception. He was a "change of speed" pitcher who continually presented the problem of timing to the batsman.

In the final analysis, control is the prime requisite of a pitcher. If he has a great assortment of pitches and moves the ball around—pitching to spots, as they say—it all depends on control. If he has all the natural stuff in the world he still must get the ball over the plate to get the most batters out and hold the opposition to a low run total.

The greatest qualification of a pitcher is the same as the greatest qualification of a hitter or of a ballplayer in any position, the same qualification of a manager or a coach or the president of a ball club or the President of the United States—he has to want to do it, to do it so much that nothing else matters.

I say there is a reason for wildness. My thinking goes in the direction that most wildness in normal men is due to a lack of concentration on spot pitching and that is traceable to a lack of self-indictment, no real sense of the need for improvement. "I don't think that I need to be better," when, in fact, everything depends upon it.

Mr. Bob Zupke, famous coach at the University of Illinois, told me that Walter Hagen, who is reputed to be one of the greatest instructors in the field of golf, said, "A great golfer never looks at the ball." And when Bob Zupke said this to me I was amazed. Confounded. Walter Hagen said, "A great golfer picks out the spot on the balls." He said he hits a different point on the ball to get the English he wants and the direction he wants and the height he wants. Hagen says that he doesn't look at the ball; he looks at a tiny spot on the ball. I think the danger is that, when we go to throw a pitch to the plate, we take in too much territory. You see the big belly of Campanella, and you see that big umpire standing back there, and you see the hitters standing up there and the strike zone—and you see an overall picture. But you should concentrate, and pitch to a spot.

If a pitcher throws one good pitch during the whole morning, you have something to work on. Let him know it. That will give him all the incentive he needs. He too sees that he can do a certain thing. He doesn't know exactly where he placed it or what his pressure was, but he has it. He may not know exactly how he did it. He has to find that out from his own study.

One of the great stumbling blocks to the perfection of pitching is the man who gets his cart ahead of the horse—the man who looks for variety, looks for repertoire—before he has a simple, fundamental pitch upon which he can rely.

Take Hal Gregg, on our Dodgers (1943–47), for example. He is a powerful pitcher in the rough. He has a beautiful fastball, a lively change of pace on his fastball, and a corking curve. He also has a very fast-spinning, breaking change of pace on his curve. Gregg has four distinct pitches. No one could beat him if he had control. Gregg has a definition of control that varies from the definition given me by a very old pitcher who was a marvelous master of pitching. He said, "Control is not putting the ball over the outside or the inside, or pitching it high or low. To me, control is throwing a strike when you have to."

It is a fear complex that makes men afraid to come through with a certain pitch. He might fight you with his fists; he might come back at you with word boldly enough. He has a lack of that thing that comes out of experience or comes out of inheritance or super-confidence in his own pitching skills. This lack causes him to be fearful that that fellow will hit this ball out of the lot if he gets it over. And so it is a ball. And then, with a modicum of timidity, he perhaps pitches a strike. He doesn't belong in the major leagues any more than I do. That kind of pitcher has to go to the minor leagues until he says, "They don't hit it." There suddenly comes upon him a realization that he can afford to give it. He must give stuff to it; but he is not pitching to weakness. He is pitching to the center, navel high, through the eight and a half inches from either side of the plate. He aims on his first one out of election, rather than on the third one out of compulsion. That is a different kind of aiming.

PROSPECTS AND SUSPECTS **Sandy Koufax** ♦ This boy comes nearest to perfection in pitching as anyone in either major league at the present time. He has more speed than Spahn and almost perfect control of a slow curve, that really curves. He also has an exceptional fastball and occasionally throws a change-up off the fastball. He has four different pitches. The best thing about Koufax, that really makes him a great pitcher, is that he uses all four, three of them constantly. This fellow has so much stuff and has such perfect control that I am almost compelled to believe that the way to beat him is to let everybody hit every cripple even to the point where our extra base hitters would hit with three and none. Koufax is not likely to walk anybody. This is the first time in six-odd years that I have ever said anything of this sort about an opposing pitcher. *Sandy Koufax had a 165-87 record in 12 major-league seasons and compiled a nearly 3-1 ratio of strikeouts to walks. He is in the Hall of Fame.*

Do you have any idea how many in the major leagues favor fast-ball pitching over curve-ball pitching? More for the fastball, let me assure you, and it begins when your daddy said, "How hard can you throw the ball?" And it continues at every level of play.

Everything in a pitcher's mind tells him he must be able to throw the ball hard, that it's his great pitch.

But go watch [Dodger lefthander] Preacher Roe sometimes. He will pitch a game that will be 50-50, or even 75-25 curve balls to fast-balls.

Oh, it's marvelous to possess a change-of-pace pitch, providing that you use it. But once they hit it, you forget about it for the rest of the game, thinking, "I'd better not throw it any more." You don't do that with a fastball when it is hit. You come back again with it.

There's a subtle little reason for that. The fastball, if it's exceptionally fast and alive, is a strikeout pitch. And you've got confidence in yourself built around the effectiveness of that pitch every time you strike out a great hitter.

When you don't strike many men out on the change of pace, you don't think confidently.

It's the reason Mr. [John] McGraw came to control every pitch because he said to me, "If you let 'em alone, they'll all throw fast ones." So he called every pitch, and pretty soon he became known as a curve-ball manager.

We don't do it enough. If you've got control of a curve ball, then use it, particularly since most hitters believe that you will go to the fastball when you're in the hole and they are looking for that pitch. You know well enough that surprise is in your favor when you cross them up with a curve ball or a breaking ball.

Lack of control, generally speaking, is a fault above the shoulders—a lack of concentration. I say generally because men can have short fingers or faulty points of contact because of the way that they hold the ball. But the average pitcher who is wild is so because of a lack of concentration on spot pitching. He does not throw the ball at a pin-point. I don't think he ever thinks: "I'm going to hit a certain spot."

But if I were to put a thousand dollar bill on home plate and place a metal coin atop the bill, and tell the pitcher that if he threw within six inches directly over that coin, he would get the bill, don't tell me that fellow's going to throw that ball eight feet high each time. You know that he's going to concentrate on that money and the spot, and will say, "Oh Lord, every ball I throw, I can make $1,000, and in the next six throws, I can make $6,000. That's pretty easy for me."

He looks at home plate, and looks at the money. He isn't thinking about the hitter or the umpire or the crowd or where anything is. Nor he doesn't see home plate 17 inches wide. He sees a little metal object right in a very specific part of the plate, and he concentrates on it, and he aims the ball to come within six inches directly over the spot.

There are three kinds of pitchers in the major leagues. The first kind gives the batsman a problem with stuff. He makes it hard to get the middles of the bat and ball to meet. He is a speedster, a strikeout artist. He has "stuff," managers call it.

The second class are pitchers, not throwers. They have superb control and are expert in varying velocity. A batsman anticipates a certain speed, starts his swing, but finds that the ball is not yet up to the plate.

The third group is simply a combination of the first two. All pitchers should try to belong to this class.

A combination of three factors determines the variables of all pitches. The first is velocity; the second is direction of the spin of the ball, and the third is the speed of the spin. A fourth is sometimes added by some college coaches (who, as a class, are more informed and more pedagogically able than most professional managers)—namely, angle of delivery. Leaving out the angle of delivery, all pitches depend on the relationship of any one of the three to either of the others, or, indeed, to both of the others. Change in velocity, combined with the same spin direction, can produce a change-up off the fastball. The same velocity when combined with different spin directions will give either the fastball or the curve. The same velocity—with changes in both spin speed and spin direction—give fadeaways or sliders. The same velocity and no defined spin direction or indeed none at all may, by intent, produce knuckleballs. If, then, the speed of the spin and its direction are combined with changes of velocities, obviously different different pitches are effected and a myriad of them are produced.

PROSPECTS AND SUSPECTS **Dave Debusschere** ♦ Shows no control of any pitch. A really remarkable delivery. If this boy had a change of speed of the fastball and had control of it, he would need only two pitches. *Dave Debusschere pitched for the Chicago White Sox in 1963 and 1964 and had a 3-4 record. He helped the New York Knicks win two NBA championships and was general manager for several years after his major-league career.*

First, let it be said that any lefthanded pitcher who allows a big lead or the advantageous break to the baserunner is either grossly stupid or doesn't care enough, or both. Because the lefthander has command of the base runner, he is in a position to say, "Heads I win, tails you lose." If the runner breaks, he is caught off. If he does not break, there is no stolen base. Over the years, many lefthanded pitchers were masters of the runners on first base—Warren Spahn, Whitey Ford, Nick Altrock of yore, Sherrod Smith of Brooklyn's ancient days.

Some years ago an allegedly "great" scientist wrote an article stating there is no such thing as a curve ball—that it was an illusion. This scientist stated that a ball that curves when it is thrown, violates the law of physics, and so on.

I don't want to debate the point with him. I don't care how scientific he may be in the whole theory of physics. The gentleman certainly never held a bat in his hand and faced Clem Labine or a dozen others just like him. He never was a catcher signalling to Rex Barney for a fastball or a curve and then found that he had been crossed up because Barney forgot the signals and he got the other pitch instead.

Just let that happen to him.

Let him stand back there with one of those fellows throwing at him after he has called for a fastball—expects one to be thrown, gets set for it, and up comes that magnificent curve ball. If that scientist won't duck and move himself out of there faster than he's ever moved before, I'll eat your hat.

PROSPECTS AND SUSPECTS **Earl Fackler** ♦ In the first half-dozen games here, he has not hit a single ball hard. Looks like he runs very good, his arm is not bad, but his helplessness at bat is apparent to everybody. I do not understand how the fellow with his fine build, all the physical set-up, can be so utterly unproductive with a piece of wood in his hands. He could do just as well with a lead pencil. *The 6'3", 190 pound Lucky" Fackler batted a respectable .281 in 6 minor-league seasons but never with power (only 21 home runs).*

Changes of speed are calculated to upset the timing of the batsman. Changes of speed are not calculated to strike men out. They are
calculated to produce less power on the part of the batsman. He will
not have the same strength, the same impetus, the same acceleration.
He has only his arms left to hit with. You're reducing his power and
upsetting the rhythm of his swing.

The most important thing in the world to you is not whether the ball
slows up or whether it has a fast rotation or whether it curves. The
merit of the pitch itself is secondary to the character of the delivery.
Without the exact sameness in delivery, I suggest that you abandon
the pitch. You must repeat delivery.

A pitcher will not acquire greater velocity. His speed will perhaps
remain about the same throughout the years of his life. But you watch
out. He will produce deflections from a straight line that you never
dreamed of.

The pitcher needs to become a fielder as soon as he throws the ball.
He must anticipate where he must go immediately. How quick can he
protect? What kind of fielder is he? More depends on the pitcher than
on anybody else.

One of the great ways to correct a pitcher who lets a runner get a good
break on a pitch is to correct the action of the left shoulder (for
righthanded pitchers) by turning it more, and making the pitcher
turn his head more. Make the pitcher look out of the corner of his
eye. He can tell where the runner is through his peripheral vision. If
his shoulder is back too far, he's too toward the far front. You may

even have to move his left foot and turn him around. But that shoulder must come around, because it's the thing that is tipping off that runner that he is going to pitch the ball home.

◇

God was responsible for Walter Johnson. His speed made it impossible to see the ball at times.

◇

Matty (Christy Mathewson) was a pitcher—the pitcher—for any given game.

◇

On the correct way to step and follow through when delivering a pitch: A pitcher's stepping habit (when he delivers a pitch) is hard to change. The foot that stays in contact with the rubber is called the pivot foot; the other foot is called the stepping foot. Some men move their feet incorrectly when they make a pitch. The difference between a poor and good fielding pitcher is in the moving of the pivot foot. Don Newcombe (Dodger pitcher 1949–58) brings himself into a beautiful fielding position every time. He steps and then, boom—he brings over his pivot foot even with his stepping foot, in perfect balance. Unfortunately, some pitchers leave their pivoting foot dangling in mid-air, and heaven help them if the ball is hit back through the box. Pitchers must be told that if they want to be great fielders, they must take that second step with the pivot foot, even if they jump at the finish of the pitch, just so long as they are balanced. It will become a habit—and an asset. It can be the difference between winning or losing the pennant.

◇

About all the scoring ever done off Dizzy Dean in his heydey was due to his jocularity, his carelessness, his momentary indifference, his knowing he "had 'em beat."

There are a hundred ways to suggest how to throw change-of-speed and change-of-pace curves and knuckleballs with one, two, or three fingers. I've gone through some of them in my coaching experience, and there are some of them that are alright. You'll find a man now and then who will not change how he places his fingers on the ball, and he'll throw a curve ball, fastball and change-of-pace with exactly the same fingering.

I've seen a number of pitchers who will get an effective change-of-pace curve ball simply by changing the pressure they place on the ball. A fellow can't have an effective change-of-pace without doing something to the position of the ball in his hand. That's the rule.

A young fellow learning to pitch a change-of-pace should answer two questions: Is it protected from detection? Is it easily acquired?

Just raising the fingers on the pitch is the best thing. Just lift the tips of the fingers off the ball and throw the fastball or curve ball, and it will be a change-of-pace, and it cannot be detected.

If the change-of-pace on the fastball is still too fast, tell the pitcher to get more of the fingers off. The ball will go high and northeast for a righthander, and high and northwest for a lefthander. Whenever the time comes that a man can throw a ball within a two-and-a-half-foot radius, don't change his position, because, if he can throw five out of six, you know he's regular and he will come to it. If the speed is too much, you can reduce it by putting the ball back in the hand little by little, and somewhere you will get it right. While moving it back, if he is a righthander, get off ten or twenty feet to the right in front of him and ask to throw fastball, change-of-pace, fastball, change-of-pace. Tell him you're watching the delivery and not the speed. He must not make a change in his delivery. Now, if he has the same delivery, you work on the velocity of the pitch.

On the curve ball, the same thing applies. Keep the delivery the same. If he doesn't get control of it by taking his fingers off, put the ball back in the hand. About half of the pitchers will get a change-of-pace curve that way.

PROSPECTS AND SUSPECTS **Vernon Law** ♦ A big righthanded Pittsburgh pitcher. Good fastball, good curve, good change-of-pace curve. He has a change of pace on his fastball with a wiggle-waggle, half fadeaway rotation. But it is definitely not a fadeaway. The only effect I see on his change-up on the fastball is in its velocity. It has no spin and no correct rotation. The velocity is reduced over his fastball, but again, not enough. He had some trouble reducing velocity, but for one out of every four or five pitches, he would get a beautiful change of pace. He can pitch on our club all right, and he can pitch his present change of speed—but not anywhere near as effective as it should be. I thoroughly believe that with some practice on the conventional change-up on the fastball, he will be much more effective. He certainly is an intelligent gentleman, and a fine character. *Vernon Law had a 162-147 record during 16 major-league seasons, 1950–67.*

On greatness: Baseball greatness is not limited to position. It will assert itself on any part of the diamond when the great player sees a chance for victory. He will find a way to beat you. That's why he is great.

CHAPTER FOUR

The Little Things

*B*eyond the basics, Rickey felt that once the game started, certain skills gave some clubs an advantage. Here he discusses base-stealing, bunting, the art of catching, and signals.

Many people are well educated theoretically with regard to baseball. They know the history of baseball from Roman times on down through Father [Henry] Chadwick to Bill Dickey's World Series home run; they know the game's rules and regulations as well as Judge Landis; they are able to tuck their trousers at the knee with as queer a flair as the dressiest professional; they have physical strength, health and good habits and even aptitude. But, they cannot play ball. No manager would use them on any professional team. No club owner would want them as coaches or managers. They are full of theory, but they have not contacted the field. They don't "click" as players.

On Basestealing

Hitting alone will not win ball games. I want speed on my team and I also want every man on the squad to know how to slide.

On a baserunner getting a good break from first when stealing: Part of the ability to get a break is born in you, but you can fortify yourself with information. Study the opposing pitchers. Take note of the pitchers' characteristic peculiarities and idiosyncracies. Talk with your team-mates about their moves. Study them while sitting on the bench. Watch and learn what it is that indicates when a pitcher is going to throw to the plate. Study all these things. Be armed with this information when you get on base. Don't hang around the bench gassing about something with one eye on your next cud of tobacco and the other on the grandstand.

I'm sure I have had some responsibility in choosing teams with good legs. Always the team had speed of foot. I'm unable to tolerate a team that cannot run. And I have given you the reason for it. In the last five years I think the records show this. For example, stolen bases. Don't misunderstand me about the meaning of stolen bases as indicating speed. The speed of a club is one of the boons along the pathway of the whole season's work that they have a stolen-base record. The stolen base is a by-product of speed.

Prior to the early thirties, basestealing was an art much studied and much practiced. Prior to that time, one player on any and all clubs stole as many bases and usually more than an entire ball club in recent years. But less drilling and instruction are given to players at the present time than was given when a stolen base was an attractive suspense feature of practically every game. And, on account of the non-enforcement of the balk rule, baserunning has all but lost the attractive feature of basestealing.

Still, the stolen base is the prolific breeder of partisanship and a frequent game determinative, and certainly one of baseball's most enthralling features. The genius of Alexander Cartwright in fixing the 90-foot distance between bases as adapted to the pitching move and the catcher's throw becomes apparent in the stolen base. The ever-present physical hazard, the unfaulty tag, the elusive slide, the violent impact, the effort of the baseman to avoid the spike, the anticipated, doubtful call that confronts any umpire—all this makes a conspiracy of so many incidents. Taken together, it produces an instantaneous single effect: The umpire's decision of "out" or "safe" makes the stolen base a high suspense moment.

The relative indifference shown today in the major leagues for the stolen base has robbed the game of one of its most dramatic moments. Every effort should now be made to preserve the stolen base, including the enforcement of the balk rule and the proper training of able base runners.

PROSPECTS AND SUSPECTS **Lou Brock** ♦ Chicago Cubs outfielder. Lefthanded all the way. A good runner and a good power hitter. Twenty-three years old. This boy is highly desirable on any major-league club. He can do everything and should hit .300. (5/1/63) *Lou Brock, playing with the Cubs and St. Louis Cardinals, batted .293 over 19 seasons. When he retired (1979), he was baseball's all-time stolen base leader, with 938. He is in the Hall of Fame.*

The lead off first—and, indeed, any base—is determined by the baserunner's knowledge of the pitcher's move and his willingness to use every inch of his lead. There can be a "one-way lead," as it is called, where the baserunner increases his lead, having in mind that, regardless of the pitcher's move, he is going back to the bag. The reason for a one-way lead, sometimes, is to get acquainted with the pitcher's move; or it could conceivably be used to cause the catcher to call for a pitch-out, thinking that the runner is likely to go. Or it could well be used occasionally to draw a throw and thus break up the pitcher's concentration on his next pitch. No manager recommends it as a part of general practice.

A baserunner is censurable if he repeatedly takes simply a one-way lead. It would mean that he makes his "break" backwards. He becomes more censurable when he loses his sense of adventure in making his break. I don't know of a really good baserunner or a good basestealer who does not have any chance-taking in his system.

There is hardly any excuse in the majors for cowardly baserunning. Shortstop Wills of the Los Angeles club should turn red the faces of twenty men in the National League who can run as fast as he can. I knew a National League outfielder who had all the skills to steal as many bases as he wished but one season stole just four.

What is the difference between his output and the 104 stolen by Wills?

Then there is the matter of sliding, another great asset in baserunning. Skill in sliding is a matter of practice. Many of the major-league's baserunners steal an imaginary base 93 feet from first base at the same time they touch the 90-foot bag at second. For example, in a slide to the right, the right foot erroneously goes past the second base bag two to five feet, in advance of the touch-down foot. This requires practice to change the direction and body position of the take-off when starting the slide. Sliding is practiced in most spring training camps very little. It is a sad commentary. The sliding pits are prepared but not used.

Running straight, a base turn, the "lead," the "break," and skillful sliding make even an average runner a feared baserunner. And the artistry in proficient baserunners affords captivating appeal to the knowing fan throughout the country.

On the Bunt

There's a marked difference between the sacrifice and the safe-hit bunt. I wish men in batting practice would do more of the safe-hit bunting than they do of the sacrifice style.

The key is not to tip off the safe-hit bunt. Some men start so fast for first base in an effort to safe hit a bunt that they become inaccurate. You can't bunt with the same procedure as when you're sacrificing. And you shouldn't. A sacrifice means sacrifice. You're giving yourself up. And even then, there's no reason to let everybody know you're going to do it. It's a marvelous thing in the tactics of our game to continually take your adversary by surprise. It almost justifies any violation of the orthodoxy of tactics.

Some men can make a sacrifice bunt better by stepping. Some men will not move either foot. I don't care when you step or if you don't step at all; that hasn't got a thing to do with it. The big end of the bat has everything to do with it. When the ball leaves a pitcher's hand, and particularly at the time that the stepping foot of the pitcher hits the ground—at that time or immediately preceding it, you try to make the big end of the bat the nearest thing to the pitcher. About that time, the thing you've got about you—your person, your bat, your foot, whatever you have—is the big end of the bat. If you don't have the big end of the bat out, what have you got to do? You've got to go forward with the bat. Bunting is a backward motion. Bunting is resistance to a pitch, and velocity determines your resistance. With a fastball, you've got to give it greater resistance, greater firmness, than you do on a change-of-pace pitch. The only way you can come back on a pitch is to have the big end out. If you've got that position in bunting, you or anybody can learn to bunt.

I know six fellows on the Brooklyn baseball club who will take a position that says "I'm going to bunt, get ready. He hasn't pitched yet, but I'm going to bunt." I can't tell you how sick that makes me. Doesn't he want to win? Please, Mr. Manager, won't you see that men in this camp bunt and bunt; but don't have them go out ahead of time.

I'm not a great believer in hit-and-run tactics. The way it is generally practiced, the hit-and-run loses many more games than it wins. There are times when it should be used. There are men who ought to be given freedom of it and there are men who ought to be made to use it, and there are times in the whole field of tactics that it should be generously employed. I understand that. But, in general use, more is lost by the hit-and-run than is gained by it.

Catcher: The Field General

The catcher is in position to be the field general. He sees exactly where seven men are standing and he should be the master defensive tactician of the game. He should be able and willing not only to select the pitch but to indicate where it should go. It is a great day for a catcher when he comes to have sufficient confidence to assert himself in moving this fielder or that, in or out or over, even to the point of stopping the game at a critical time and having a talk with the team captain or even the manager. A great catcher like Campanella or [Mickey] Cochrane or [Bill] Delancey or [Johnny] Kling or [Bill] Dickey practically runs the game.

With a runner on base anywhere, every dirt pitch should be body-checked. The catcher is never a shortstop on ground pitches, and it is almost criminal for a catcher to try to handle such pitches only with the glove. The catcher should drop to both knees, with his hands, arm, and body making as wide a target for the pitch as possible and with no chance to let the ball go through him.

You cannot win a pennant with a poor catcher. And how often the best catcher in baseball is in the World Series! A pennant winner must be strong everywhere, and this strength starts behind the plate.

PROSPECTS AND SUSPECTS **Bill Mazeroski** ♦ This kid has a good arm. Looks to be 6'0", 175 pounds, and is 17 years of age. He can throw sidearm, underhand, and overhand. Has good body control. From a fielding standpoint, he is definitely a prospect. Hardly strides at all. Wonderful. Changes of speed should not bother him very much and eventually it will never bother him. What he will do with the curve ball with deflections, I don't know. He hits at bad balls, as all kids do; but he plays the ball well wherever pitched. Good power—not great, but good. I would definitely consider him a prospect. *(1954)*
Bill Mazeroski batted .260 and had a .983 fielding average during 17 major-league seasons.

Team Defense

Fielding may be comparatively insignificant if the opposing club cannot make any runs off your pitcher. But even the greatest pitching can be hampered by individual fielding faults. Consider these technical misfeasances (which add up to malfeasances):

Catchers who do not shift both feet on all pitches, or who do not body check on all direct pitches with a runner on base anywhere are defective fielding catchers.

Pitchers who cannot hold runners on base, allow stolen bases usually attributed improperly by many fans and some official scorekeepers to be bad catching, are poor defenders. Worse than that are the pitchers who allow their bodies to fall extremely to the right or left in following through on the pitch. The ball hit through the box or behind him becomes a base hit.

The first baseman who takes the throw from his catcher and turns to his left to tag the runner seldom gets anybody.

A second baseman who unbalances his body by shifting his weight right or left on the call of the pitching signal becomes "dumb" in trying to be smart.

The shortstop who may never have learned the splendid detail, basically mechanical, in holding runners on second base puts a run across the plate on a puny single.

The infielder who tags six inches above the ground instead of on the ground is a faulty fielder.

The third baseman who plays the line or shortly back of it on a dead left field power hitter even when the call is two strikes reminds me of a New York Knickerbockers second baseman of 75 years ago who played all the time with his foot on the second base bag.

Outfielders who take the double step after catching a fly ball seldom throw out anybody although they may have marvelous arms with correct trajectory. It is called "running with the ball."

I get so impatient with the men who know better and don't do better; who can do it and know that they should do it and will still continue to violate every correct principle of a play.

Take the trajectory of an outfielder's throw. It should be the same as the catcher's throw to second base but we have outfielders who throw that ball up so that, three out of four times, a relay man at 180 feet can't get it.

Now it isn't the point that he deprives the infielder of the right of the judgment on the cut-off, and where the play should go, and what other men behind him are telling him. The outfielder says, "I'm not going to let you fellows exercise your brains on this play. I'm going to deprive all of you." So he just throws it over that man all the time.

But not only does that outfielder deprive the team of exercising its best judgment, he also defeats himself because that ball, with its high trajectory as opposed to the low trajectory from him to the infielder, will not go as fast.

Outfielders should not throw more than 200 feet from the cut-off man, or so on the first bounce, you see the rotation of the ball and what deflection of that first bounce means. Did it hop into the air? Did it shoot along the ground? There's where you judge speed and the effectiveness of an outfielder's arm.

Often the ball's rotation is completely wrong. It should be directed back toward him just the same as the catcher's arm.

On the Balk

The balk rule is just as basic and organic to the game as any other rule.

It was written about 100 years ago by Alexander Cartwright. It was adopted by the National League in 1876, also by the American League when it was organized in 1901.

The thrust of the rule was to allow a baserunner to take a lead from his base and have some mobility to break off the pitcher's move to the plate, in order to run successfully to the next base. This would be called a "stolen base."

> ". . . If there is a runner, or runners, it is a balk when the pitcher delivers the pitch from set position without coming to a stop."

The rule was observed for the first 60 or 70 years, and during that period the stolen base was an interesting suspense feature of the game. Then the home run craze largely brought about by Babe Ruth had a full part in creating an army of puny hitters to try from infancy to hit an over-the-fence trajectory—an upswing at the ball. Waiting for the power stroke reduced the stolen bases.

Then came gradually the "non-stop" era in pitching. Lax enforcement by umpires resulting from loose interpretation of what constituted a "stop" followed.

For sometime prior to 1950, there was practically no stop. The violation became almost relatively flagrant yet frequent and baseball demanded some kind of change. The Rules Committee in 1950 (of which I was a member) undertook to do something about it and what ensued were lengthy discussions about defining a "stop." The Committee solved it, or so it thought, by simply adding four words to the original rule: ". . . of one full second," so that it read:

> ". . . If there is a runner, or runners, it is a balk when the pitcher delivers the pitch from set position without coming to a stop of one full second."

The Committee agreed that "one full second" could be measured vocally by uttering the words "one thousand and one."

Alexander Cartwright evidently thought that "stop" meant stop. His idea obviously of a stop was to give sufficient time for the runner to jockey from his lead and break. I think he would have opposed a limitation defined by saying "a thousand and one."

It was agreed that baserunning was desirable; that it had become a lost art. For part of the ensuing season, the "one full second rule" followed but then sagged back to almost non-enforcement.

Every player, except pitchers, knew that an observable pause in the pitcher's delivery enabled the baserunner to balance his weight and perhaps give him time to increase his lead. Non-enforcement simply puts the pitcher at an advantage.

The doubtful ethics of teaching pitchers how to violate the rule with loose enforcement in vogue provided increased violations and this in turn resulted in extensive abandonment of managerial directives of the "stolen base."

But without enforcement, where are we?

As the balk stands now, coaches are encouraged to study means and methods by which to cheat and cheapen the rule. Baseball is simply patting the criminal on the back of the hand and saying, "Sorry to have bothered you a bit." They didn't even admonish the culprit to "go and sin no more." They sent the violating pitchers to heaven without repentance. St. Peter will have something to say to somebody about that. *(1963)*

PROSPECTS AND SUSPECTS **Ralph Kiner** ♦ He would not throw or run and could not field and was a self-appraised star and could have no part ever in a pennant winning club. Kiner was a gentleman and a fine person but I cannot be any respecter of persons, nor character nor anything else when it comes to winning a pennant. *(1952) Kiner led the major leagues in home runs, averaging 42 per year, for seven consecutive years. He finished his 10-year career second only to Babe Ruth in home run percentage (averaging slightly more than seven home runs per 100 at bats).*

Breaking the Code

The U.S. government broke down the Japanese code, but it took them thousands of workers and experts. We are not going into anything that intricate, so it is easy to break down the signals of another club. It is easy to steal signals.

From the standpoint of a manager, the best thing is to conceal the source of the signal so the opponent won't know where it's coming from. If you want to steal signals, the first and most important thing is to find the source of signals.

When at bat or on base, a smart baseball player will always wait until one subsequent act after the signal to carry out. Let the man giving the signal make another motion before you look away. Acknowledging a sign prematurely will allow signals to be stolen. The player makes the signal safe.

I have sometimes said a team that continues to miss signals is never to blame. That is the manager's fault. There's something wrong with the education of the man—and most particularly with the charter of the signals.

Signals are important. A manager who doesn't have control of his hitters and is unable to change a situation when he wants to doesn't have control of the game. If the manager changes his mind for one reason or another, he must have a simple device for getting his change up to the batter. I suggest that the way to do this is to call every man by two names. Say it's Bill Smith and everybody calls him Bill, but when someone calls him Smith, he must step out of the batter's box and look at the coach or manager. When you use a man's last name, there is no confusion and you can stop a man whenever you want to. And you have a quick way by which you can change the bunt to freedom to hit, or vice versa. Managers must also have variations on the basic signals. These are signals which you give in certain situations. Suppose you have a signal for a sacrifice bunt and you signal the batter to bunt on the first pitch, but only if it is a strike. The pitch is high and outside—a ball—and now you want him to hit free because the first and third basemen have left their positions before the pitch was delivered. Don't give him the "hit free" signal, give him the "cross" signal, which tells the batter to do the opposite of what you last wanted him to do. This confuses the opposition. They are looking for you to give either the bunt or the "hit free" signal. Even if they see the "cross" signal they won't know for certain what it is you want the batter to do.

Cultivating Skills

Mr. Rickey did not believe in mindless practice, he advocated practice with intent. One of his early successes was helping St. Louis Cardinal outfielder Austin McHenry (1918–22), cut down on his excessive strike-out rate against righthanded pitchers (in 1920–73 SO in 504 official AB): Austin worked for several days against the human arm, hitting approximately 100 pitches each forenoon. At week's end, he came to me after practice and asked, "What's this all about?" I'm hitting outside pitches to right field and inside pitches to left field. I asked him a question in return, "Mac, do you recall how many pitches you missed today?" After a moment of hesitation, he replied that he did not miss any. "And how many did you miss yesterday?" No reply quickly, and I said, "Very few, and when this new effort of bringing yourself to mastery of hitting the ball where it's pitched becomes habit, I don't believe you will strike out so much." He became a batsman with a normal record of striking out (in 1921, 48 SO in 574 AB). If you care enough to improve, always practice with intent.

If a man wants to do something and you want to help him, give him an objective. This is true in cultivating skills in any profession.

PROSPECTS AND SUSPECTS **Eddie Stanky** ♦ He can't hit, he can't run, he can't field and he can't throw, but if there's a way to beat the other team, he'll find it. *(about 1947) The Brat was a pest—he led the National League three times in bases on balls, averaging 143, almost one per game, and compiled a respectable .268 lifetime batting average over his 11-year major-league career.*

CHAPTER FIVE

Back to
the Future

Rickey wanted to win, yet at the same time save money and the energy of his players and his scouts. Out of this desire came his constant drive to bring innovation to the game, to use new ideas and inventions and keep baseball moving forward. Some of his contributions changed baseball forever.

Scouting: Dollar Sign on Muscle

Upon seeing for the first time then minor-league pitching prospect and future Hall-of-Famer, Chick Hafey, blast a long ball over the fence: From now on he's an outfielder.

"High School Rule." Back in the early fifties, major-league baseball had a rule prohibiting a team from even discussing a professional career with a promising player who still had high school eligibility remaining. It was called simply the "High School Rule," which came about because teams had signed high school players and sent them off to the minor leagues before they graduated and thus completed their eligibility.

At first I had no objection to the rule, but soon it became obvious that it could not be enforced. Nothing made less sense than having an unenforceable rule on the books. So, after the 1951 season, while I was general manager of the Pittsburgh Pirates, Amendment No. 106 was proposed: "Nothing herein shall be construed as prohibiting any major- or minor-league club, its officers, agents, or employees from talking to any high school student at any time concerning a career in professional baseball and discussing the merits of his contracting, when eligible therefore, with any particular club."

In my view, that amendment permitted any club or its agent to talk to any boy about a career in professional baseball and to discuss the terms of a contract. What the amendment did forbid was signing the boy to a contract.

What I really favored was Amendment No. 107, proposed by the Rochester club. It provided abolition of the current rule and everything pertaining to it, and permitted the signing (but not the use) of any high school player until his graduation. This guaranteed that all high school teams could retain their identity, knowing full well that a player contemplating a professional career will be eligible until his graduation.

It also bothered me that people believed that a boy who signed a professional contract that made him ineligible under the present rule was of lesser moral character, and that it was wrong for his father or a designated advisor to negotiate a future contract while the boy was still in high school. Amendment No. 107 simply says to all parties that "we will not give the boy employment until after the date of his graduation."

Now there is another good reason to be rid of the High School Rule as written or proposed: It promotes the "bonus," and that is the greatest menace to the continued solvency of a great many major-league teams. Some teams are spending as much as a half-million dollars yearly in signing new, young, untried players about whose ability nothing positive is known. The bonus inherently affects the player in a number of negative ways. The player's morale is upset. He is often ruined by the sudden possession of large amounts of money. His ambition is stultified. And his self-sufficiency is pronounced (even his habits in the direction of the "good life" are affected).

The club is likewise affected, because it is just too bad to have 25-year-old, tried and true players view with amazement the presence of one or even a half-dozen bonus players who get more money to sign a contract as an 18-year-old than most of them can ever hope to save in a lifetime of playing.

The financial structure of the game is jeopardized. Most clubs cannot possibly pay between $300,000 and $700,000 a year for new, unknown material of tender age and be assured of staying solvent. *Retaining the ability to sign high school talent was crucial to Rickey. It had long been a source of "cheap" players for his minor-league clubs. Players who developed into stars were promoted to the major-league club, and others were sold to other clubs to raise cash, of which a significant amount found its way into Rickey's pocket. The imposition of a rule which forbade signing high school players, or in any way tampered with the status quo that Rickey has so successfully manipulated, threatened to force Rickey to buy established players, or to pay bonus money to free agents. To Rickey, these were two decidedly unattractive and unprofitable options, and he resisted them vigorously. Rickey's prediction that high-dollar bonuses for free agents—both untested and proven—would lead to financial distress for poorer clubs is an enduring problem for major-league baseball.*

The question often is raised to me about whether a boy "likes to play." We have scouts who have that in mind, and invariably they make it a key part of their report. A scout will enthusiastically tell me about a player: I'm telling you, "He can hit a ball a 'fur piece.' He can throw the ball hard and he can run like all get-out. Branch, he loves to play." Invariably the scout tacks it on. He can't see boys who don't care to play. Sometimes I think it has to be tacked on. It's such a sad commentary on a man who is physically and materially set up for a great career in this game and has no showmanship in the field of desire to enjoy it, to want to play. There is a fellow on our club right now. He can't throw very good, not too good, can't run as fast as most of you, hasn't any great power, but he has a dominating obsession to play. He loves to play this game. First man out, last man in. Ready for anything. Alert for a chance to do something. So there is that extra thing to look for in a prospective player.

What do you look for in pitchers? Size. The big man is better than the little man. He can acquire all of the intricacies of detail and technique that the little man can, if he has the same motivation. Agility and good physical coordination. This is valuable, even if you are a dishwasher. Speed afoot? This is more or less inconsequential.

What makes you or breaks you is the ability to choose from among the in-betweens those boys who will go on to make good.

On the advantage of his 1965 proposal to pool major-league scouting departments: Each club would get the most expert information from no less than three high-class scouts (vs. one under the current system) on every prospect.

Scouting and the Tryout Camp: Many Are Called But Few Are Chosen

I believe very strongly in the local tryout camp idea for a major-league club. All the players run and are timed with a stopwatch. The comparative running speed of every player will be known and his running form correctly appraised. Everybody throws: catchers, infielders, outfielders, first basemen—everyone except pitchers. Every coach marks his own clip sheet. Evaluations are compared later. No man with a sore arm or with an ailing arm should be permitted to throw and no man should be permitted to throw without being well warmed up.

PROSPECTS AND SUSPECTS   **Don Drysdale** ♦ 6′4″, 185 pound, 18 years of age. Intelligent face and manner, shows good breeding. This boy had a high scholastic record, almost a straight A. A lot of artistry about his boy. Way above average fastball. It is really good. Placement on fastball and curve ball needs no coaching. Let him alone on all his fingering; he is good. This boy's curve is fairly good, and he shows control. He has a change-up on his curve and that is usable. He is a definite prospect. With proper handling, I could see this boy on the Pittsburgh club in two years. He impresses me very much. I would sign him to a Pittsburgh contract, for I think he would come within three years, but his first contract must not be over $4,000. If he were to stay with our club, his salary would be the minimum in the major leagues, $6,000. *Eventually, Drysdale was signed by the Brooklyn Dodgers and finished a 14-year major-league career with a 209-166 record. He is in The Hall of Fame.*

The pitcher candidates are worked individually on the sideline by an experienced person or two. Full dictation is made on all pitcher tryouts. The pitching machine and the batting cage should be employed. Batsmen are judged on stride, hand, and batting position and other details, but with particular attention on the part of all coaches to the batsman's power.

When you're eighteen years old and can't run fast, you'll never run fast. If you can't throw the ball hard at eighteen, you never will. If you haven't got a heart at eighteen, you'll never get one later on. If your morals are bad at eighteen, you'll never improve.

Above all, a scout should look for power in a hitter. You might say, "Why not hitting percentage?" No! No! No! There are so many things that interfere with the .300 hitter. He may be only .240, .250, and come to be .350. His greatness may depend on whether he has no vital faults, no violation of hitting fundamentals. He will acquire correct technique, but very few men will acquire power. You either have it, or you don't. Look for power in hitting.

Very seldom does a scout name the price that he thinks should be paid for a prospect's contract. Instead, the main office must make the decision, and it often wishes more information. It would like to have a dependable opinion from somebody else, yet you often find, the more conversation you have, the more bewilderment you meet—and one soon doesn't know what to do.

A scout may know that, from certain characteristics of a prospect, he will not go far and he acts upon that fact and doesn't recommend the player. Now, knowing that is important to me and our organization, and those facts help to better arm the organization and anybody in it who must put a dollar mark on muscle.

And that's the important thing in this business.

PROSPECTS AND SUSPECTS   **Roberto Clemente**   ♦   I have been told often from many sources about his speed, but I was sorely disappointed. His running form is bad, and based upon what I saw tonight, he has only a bit above average major-league speed. He has a beautiful throwing arm. However, he runs with the ball every time he makes a throw, and that's bad. He is not adventuresome on the bases, takes a comparatively small lead and doesn't have in mind getting a break. His form at the plate is perfect. The bat is out and back and in good position to give him power. There is not the slightest hitch or movement in his hands or arms and the big end of the bat is completely quiet when the ball leaves the pitcher's hand. His sweep is level, his stride is short, his stance is good, and he finished good with his body. I know of no reason why he should not become a very fine hitter. I would not class him, however, as even a prospective home run hitter. I do not believe he can possibly do a major-league club any good this year. In 1956, he can be sent out on option by Pittsburgh only by first securing waivers, and waivers likely cannot be secured. So we are stuck with him—stuck indeed until such time as he can really help a major-league club. *Pittsburgh was "stuck" with Clemente for 18 seasons, during which he batted .317, compiling 3,000 hits including 240 home runs. He is in The Hall of Fame. As Rickey suspected, Clemente developed slowly, batting .282 over his first 5 seasons and .330 over the remainder of his major-league career.*

There are only three fundamental things that scouts should look at when they're judging players—the arm, the legs, and power. A good strong arm: How does he throw? A pair of fast legs: Speed of foot. And power: I regard power as less important than legs, and the arm as less important than the legs.

If I were to write four units on the board as the qualities of a player, I should have to give about two points to the legs and one to the arm and one to power. Because the arm is used only defensively. The power is used only offensively. The legs are so much in evidence— both offensively and defensively.

The most difficult position player to scout is an outfielder. You may go for days and he may not hit, or he may not have an opportunity to demonstrate his arm strength. I remember very well once having a man in the American Association who—at the end of a month, following a player in his city—told me he'd never had a chance to see his arm. Well, that's possible but very improbable.

Rickey's judgment was not infallible. In 1952, he observed then Pittsburgh farm pitcher Ron Necciai and remarked: "I've seen a lot of baseball in my time. There have only been two young pitchers I was certain were destined for greatness, simply because they had the meanest fastball a batter can face. One of those boys was Dizzy Dean. The other is Ron Necciai. And Necciai is harder to hit." *Necciai pitched only one season for the Pirates and finished with a record of 1 and 6. He left baseball with an ERA of 7.08. However, Necciai still holds the professional baseball record for strikeouts in one game, 27, for Bristol in the Appalachian League.*

PROSPECTS AND SUSPECTS   Jim Hayden ♦ "How old are you, Jim," I said, when I met him on the mound this morning at the start of my workout.

"Well," he said, "I am 20."

"When will you be 21?"

"In July."

"What day in July?"

"Let's see," said he, "the 11th of July."

"This is the 13th," I said.

He said, "of July?"

I said, "yes, July."

"Not July?"

"Yes, this is July, and this is the 13th of July."

"Well, I must have had a birthday the day before yesterday."

Tall, slim, lefthander, naïve as the dickens. "Are you married Jim?"

"No, I ain't."

"Are you about to be?"

"No, but I am in sort of a mess though."

"Oh, is that so. What about?"

"About this damn curve ball."

"What's that got to do with your girl, if anything?"

"Girl—who said anything about a girl. What I'm talking about is the mess with this curve ball. That's the only thing that worries me!"

(7/13/55) Lefthander Jim Hayden never did master the curve ball. He toiled for five years, 1954–1958, in the low minors before ending his professional baseball career.

Build It and They Will Come: The Farm System

The farm system, which I have been given credit for developing, originated from a perfectly selfish motive: saving money.

Many have seen it quite properly as a great means of developing players and making a team a consistent contender; but that was simply a by-product.

When I first went to St. Louis with Mr. [Robert Lee] Hedges, who owned the Browns, he convinced me that no team could compete for players in the marketplace with big-city teams like New York and Chicago, and often Pittsburgh, whose "transient" attendances alone—those from people just visiting those cities—were equal to our permanent and transient attendance.

Those were the teams that pretty much were ruling the game back in the late teens and throughout the twenties.

There were minor leagues all over the country owned by people in individual communities. They signed players and trained them, hoping that those who became stars would be attractive on the open market and fetch nice prices from the teams above them, right up to the major leagues.

So they were as anxious to be supported by a major-league team as we were to take advantage of having our players on distinct teams—and not have to go pay exorbitant prices in the open market.

We tried an arrangement in Houston, Texas, but the ownership changed hands and it never worked out. We bought our first team in 1921, a Class D team in Fort Smith, Arkansas. We had Syracuse, of the International League, on a 50-50 basis, but that proved to be a bad experience. Then we had 95 percent of the Houston team, with an option to buy the other five percent. So, of the first three teams we owned, one was in Class D [Ft. Smith], one was in Class AA [Syracuse] and the other one was in Class A [Houston].

Now, this cost us some money; but we tried to run it so we would break even. It was a cost of producing players. If it was going to cost more than purchasing players, it was out. If we could break even, it looked like a great saving, for it meant a plan that would enable the parent club to secure talent at practically no cost.

It seemed to me that the system not only gave us our raw material at less cost, but we also had an exclusive selection of better material than the average club could get on the open market. It was then a question of selecting cities that made money or broke even. The latter was difficult because it was an expensive investment to start with. So I built the St. Louis farm system largely from cities that no one else wanted to operate—or indeed, would operate.

The money part aside, the system offered a selection of better players. We knew our own material; we had followed it for several years. We brought it along to each level. That justified a larger scouting staff, which meant more players were signed and put in the proper area of competition. We controlled the instruction and discipline, and we had a much better idea of a player's major-league ability than if we had gone blindly into the open market.

Once I had all six clubs in the Nebraska State League. I also had the Arkansas State League. Once, we had about 27 clubs owned or with whom we had a working arrangement. They required financial assistance and talent, but this paid off for the Cardinals in 1923 and 1925, and we had a great team in 1926—all home grown.

I believe the farm system is definitely right, first on the ground of efficiency in operation; second on its in-bred economy; and third, on the marvelous promotional programs that you can get from it from finding and developing raw material. It is the only promotional program I can think of that has in it the wide extension of interest in organized baseball in developing young talent. It is high class. It is a frontal attack. It is wide open, progressive, efficient and healthy.

I'm still for it as a program, because I think it serves the interest of a great many communities that could not otherwise have baseball.

The development of a major league club on any permanent basis should involve planning not only for one succeeding season but for the permanency of a proud position in all succeeding season.

Without the minor leagues, baseball can get nowhere. When the majors get to the point where they think they do not have to consider the status of the minors, then a great danger exists to the structure of baseball. The St. Louis Cardinals' minor league interests are two-to-one over our major league interests and we are the National League champions (1930).

The development of the farm system was a case of necessity being the mother of invention. We lived a precarious existence. We would trade one player for four and then sell one of them for some extra cash. We were always at a distinct disadvantage, trying to get players from the minor leagues. Other clubs would outbid us; they had the money and the superior scouting machinery. *The National Agreement of 1921, which granted major-league clubs the right to own minor-league franchises, paved the way for Rickey's creation of a farm system.*

On the vicissitudes of pre-farm system player development: Friendship is the best thing you can have, but when a man who is your friend has controlling interest in a minor-league club dies, or sells out, then all your (oral) agreements amount to nothing.

No club should set up a farm and then hunt for the personnel with which to operate it. That is putting the cart before the horse, and that has never worked out. The number of your farms must be predicated on your need of that number. It must be regulated by the number of players whose contracts you must correct.

I feel I stimulated the playing of baseball in many small towns through the farm system. I broke down the color barrier and I instituted daily meetings among the players. They weren't taken very seriously in my time, but they are today. I always considered them an educational and instructional approach to the game.

Spring Training: A Regimented System

Rickey's 1912 Browns were the first team to take spring training in St. Petersburg, Florida. "I will have three batting cages, three handball courts, one sliding pit, and a place for running dashes. I intend to have my players taught how to run. Few players know the slightest thing about sprinting. I will teach my players how to make the hook slide to both sides. Handball will help my players to get in condition, brighten their eyes, make them alert. I don't say that we will win any pennants—no, far be it for me to mention anything of that kind—but I do think that my systematic training will be laying the foundation of a pennant winner.

It is surprising how many pennants and even World Series are won or lost in spring training camps.

In the Dodger camp, 1946: There are two things in this camp—the pitchers throw wild and the batters hit wild. They complement each other. The batter makes the pitcher look better, and the pitcher helps the batter. They both look good because they are both so bad.

Men can imitate. Men can learn. They do, but sometimes, and very often indeed, men who rely upon their own observations, initiatives, or adaptations do not improve very rapidly. Learning by imitation is a slow process. So, down here at Vero Beach, we have undertaken to do a bit of instruction: to tell men how they should do things; what the correct techniques are; what the proper practices are. We will challenge their intelligence at many points so that there will be a more rapid development of the player. We really want to contribute something to the baseball education of boys, apart from what they get by their own observation.

The educational method in baseball has given rise to the lecture room. Not all players can absorb instruction and gain proficiency from the spoken or written word. To some, the manager or coach will simply cast his breath on the desert air. However, he should employ the instruction method if he has one or more who may benefit greatly from his counsel. Even the blackboard, once so utterly ridiculed, has now become a mark among the more intelligent managers.

About 50 years ago, I went to a major-league training camp. We had bats and balls and meager equipment. We reported on the field at 10:00 A.M., and we worked until about 12:30 P.M. Everybody took a turn at bat, except pitchers. Each man would hit in turn four or five times a maximum of say, fifteen fair balls. Half of those fair hits in that day, as in this, would be hit on bad pitched balls, meaning that the balls hit fair were not pitches within the strike zone. The pitchers were soon worn out and the batting practice was over. Then we warmed up and took infield practice. Outfielders shagged for fifteen minutes and we called it a day. Thirty days of that routine completed spring training.

More men are put out of commission at spring training by side diversions or outside activities than from scheduled exercises of work afield. For example, I've had more casualties from sunburn than I've ever had from the aches and pains of early drills, and sunburns are unnecessary.

PROSPECTS AND SUSPECTS **Duke Snider** ♦ Duke Snider is going to be a great hitter when he learns the strike zone is not high and outside. (1947) *Over 18 seasons with the Dodgers, the Duke of Flatbush posted Hall-of-Fame lifetime statistics, including 407 home runs and a career .295 batting average.*

I think it is a very great mistake to limit attendance at the major-league training camp only to players on the 40-man roster. In the end, many players will save a full year, or maybe two years, by spending one full training period with the major-league club.

All players in the Cardinal organization who have a reasonable chance to make the club in 1964 should be invited to report with the so-called regular players on the first day of spring training. There are many boys who can hit-and-run and throw, but do not become oriented even if they may have come directly form AAA and with great records.

On a personal level, acquaintanceship with the manager, coaches, and players is important. Getting a feeling of at-homeness, a sense of belonging frequently enables prospective players to feel at home and enables them to play on the major field just as efficiently and in exactly the same manner as they did in the minors.

Over the years, I've seen too many boys fail to make good in the majors on their first or second trial simply because of lack of confidence. It is a wonderful thing for many kids to feel that they ought to stay with the major-league clubs at the very time they are sent back for further experience.

And it is a splendid asset to any young but great prospective player to believe in himself, believe that he is better than what is up there.

One of Mr. Rickey's simplest innovations for spring training use was the creation of a visible strike zone. He called it "pitching to the strings." Creating a visible strike zone in the pitcher's mind, regardless of where the batter may be standing in the batter's box, helps a pitcher throw to the intended spot. Here's how to install the strings. Drive two six-foot poles 12 inches into the ground, 15 feet apart. Place a home plate mid-way between the poles with the right angle apex of the plate exactly in line with the poles. Connect the poles with two parallel small strings, one shoulder high, the other knee high (top and bottom limits of the strike zone). Attach two very light strings to the top lateral string 17 inches apart, and wind the strings' bottom extensions one or two loops around the lower lateral string, the two loops also 17 inches apart. The strings attached to the poles can be moved up or down to simulate the batsmen's various strike zones. A catcher, without any equipment, can safely work behind the strings. Regardless of where a batsman stands, the strings create a visible strike zone in the pitcher's mind. Pitching to the strings will accelerate the mastery of control, and pitchers, particularly the younger ones, should be given ample opportunity to use them.

Mr. Rickey's unique way to detect good or bad throwing mechanics: Mark a ball with ink spots on both sides to establish an axial line. Ask the pitcher to place his fingers parallel to the axis and make several throws. If the ball maintains the same axis for these throws, it is safe to note that the pitcher either has control or can acquire it because he is releasing the ball consistently.

Branch Rickey's way to determine pitching aptitude: Have the pitcher alter the fingering of his curve ball, say, lifting the tips off the ball. If he can adapt himself to the altered style without too much difficulty, you can assume that this is a player who can develop new deliveries. This is a test that helps find the prospects who are in the twilight zone, those borderline cases on which you must make a prediction of future success. It's no trick to spot the greats or humpty-dumpties.

Early Radar: The Electronic Umpire

Mr. Rickey came up with an electronic umpire during the 1950 spring training season at the Brooklyn Dodgers camp in Vero Beach.

The gadget was conceived by Charley Lare, a rookie pitcher who had played for Princeton University, and further developed by engineers from General Electric. Lare designed the machine primarily to register balls and strikes, but Mr. Rickey encouraged more research to develop its capacity to measure a pitch's speed provided the pitch sailed over the plate as a strike. Thus, the Mahatma and his scouts were able to determine immediately if a phenom's fastball measured up to major-league standards.

The machine operated through a series of mirrors and electric eyes. The contrivance actually was cross-eyed (Why not? Umpires have always been accused of that malady!), with two mirrors looking skyward at 90-degree angles and a third mirror cast at a 45-degree angle, to register the flight of the ball by the shadow it cast. If the pitch was a strike, the ball was seen by the eyes in the mirror in 1-2-3 order, and electric impulses were created which lit a strike-indicating lamp.

An inside or outside pitch was not seen at all. A high or low pitch was spotted in an improper sequence, and the lamp would not light, thereby indicating it was a ball. The strikes and the speed of the pitches were recorded on a machine.

Of course, a couple of decades later, the "radar gun" came into wide use to measure the speed of pitches, but the balls and strikes were still left to the umpires.

The Pitching Machine

I regard the pitching machine as an instrument of helpfulness to almost any player in the world. Here are the advantages as I see them:

1. It can throw the ball with varying speeds. It can simulate several pitches of the human arm and produce different rotations, or none at all. But the machine can perform this function with a regularity and accuracy unattainable by the human arm. The pitching machine will never tire and start throwing sloppy pitches. In addition to the quality this gives to practice time, the batsman is never in danger of injury; the pitching machine will not send a player to the hospital.

2. Unlike a human pitcher, the machine can pitch to the batsman's weaknesses with considerable regularity, thereby allowing him a maximum amount of concentrated practice in the specific area in which he wishes to better himself.

3. The pitching machine is both economical and time-saving. A batter doesn't have to stand up to the plate for an extended time in order to hit three good balls. The batsman can be served from six to ten good pitches per minute. It does not require a catcher although one can be used, and to the great benefit of the catcher if he is unskilled. However, the 200 balls that can be pitched before gathering up enables the practice to be fast and continuous.

4. The batsman can umpire the pitches. He then can compare his decision with that of an umpire or another batsman standing behind him. The result is that after long practice from the pitching machine, he may finally come to know the strike zone. His confidence mounts because he is now able to get the count to 2 and 0 or 3 and 1, where for years he has been continuously in the hole.

5. You can judge many more batsmen in one hour of practice than you can with the human arm in one week. The pitching machine permits fast observation of many boys in a given length of time on the "step" or "stride"—and whether the rear foot moves or where or when or how it moves and whether the front foot definitely overstrides.

Because of the frequency of pitches and their control, one can tell by the time a boy finishes his second turn in the cage whether he has a level sweep and no "come up" at the end of his stroke. You can also get a good idea whether a hitter is straight away, pulls very much or pushes weakly. Stride, swing, position of the hands as related to the body, "hitches," bat position, batting-box position, stance, form, and power are all observable with the pitching machine. You can find these things out in time from the human arm, but it may take you two weeks. You can find out in one day on a pitching machine.

6. A pitching machine affords the quickest and most effective practice in both acquiring new habits and breaking bad ones. For instance, hitting to the opposite field and correcting a "hitch" is more safely and more easily practiced from the pitching machine because of the quantity of good balls pitched in a small amount of time. In addition, a player can work out alone.

7. The pitching machine tends to give confidence to batters who have none. Pitchers when they come to bat are subconsciously (some consciously) afraid of a pitched ball. From their boyhood days, they have had to pitch to batters and had less opportunity of batting. And as they progressed, they played only one out of every five days. Of course, they cannot bat as well as other players. To stand up and learn actually that the plate is not 18 inches wide but only 17; and to know where his knees and armpits are as related to the pitch; and to become unafraid as he watches the ball go by, are worthwhile accomplishments. The batter's courage mounts and it will not take very long for pitchers who assiduously apply themselves to practice on the pitching machine to come to hit and bunt with confidence and skill.

8. Bunting form can be taught against a pitching machine better than it can against a human machine because the pitches are buntable and the coaching opportunity is much better. Instructions can be given more privately and more pointedly. Good bunting can be taught to men who know nothing about it because it is capable of demonstration in simple basic form.

On the pitching machine (1946): The thing can throw twenty-five hundred baseballs a day. One pitcher averages one hundred and twenty-five pitches in a nine-inning game. This equals twenty pitchers working nine innings. And it takes only one man to operate it—and he does not have to be a pitcher . . . or even a baseball player!

Mr. Rickey continued his love affair with the pitching machine through the years. He wrote the following in 1963 (two years prior to his death). Year after year, I become more convinced that the pitching machine is the greatest time-saver—you can judge more batsmen in one hour of practice than you can with the human arm in a week, and every pitcher who practices as a batsman with the machine can learn to bunt.

Mr. Rickey developed the sliding pit to teach players how to perfect their sliding techniques without fear of injury. It was usually filled with sawdust or sand, or both, which produced a safe and soft landing. To avoid catching their cleats, players often removed their shoes. There are some jobs in baseball that are a bit difficult, and they require a little extra physical work. Sliding is one of them. The sliding pit is not meant to polish a man's skills. You cannot slide, hit the base with the extended foot, leg under so that a man can just bring himself right up to his feet, turn at right angles and continue to third or home. But it can be used to teach form and show principle without men getting hurt. It is the greatest thing for teaching the little techniques or pointing out the fault of a man's slide to the left or the right (hook slides) or the leg under (straight-in slide). It can be used to make men unafraid. It can make men think they can do it, and they will do it and save a game.

The Baseball Tee

Mr. Rickey, who had long maintained that there was no cure for an "over-strider," in 1948 finally came up with a hoped-for cure—a tee, not unlike one used by golfers, and certainly like one now used in the T-Ball Leagues for pre-Little League players.

It was several feet off the ground, made of hard rubber, and at the base it had a sensitive spring hinge that allowed the tee to bend freely toward the ground anytime a player smacked it instead of the ball. It simply snapped back into place.

Mr. Rickey once explained it:

"We set the ball up on the tee at the front of the plate—dead center, laterally, and then we tell the ballplayer to stand any place he cares in the batter's box. Most of them stand well to the rear because it has been proven that the maximum hitting power is obtained by making contact with the ball well out in front of the bat. But in order to strike the ball up front, the batter cannot stride past the point of contact. Hitting at this stationary ball automatically seems to cut down the step taken by natural overstriders."

It was the final link to a lifetime of "cures" for overstriders, beginning with a circular wooden rim that he developed while coaching at Ohio Wesleyan. "It was similar to one used by shot-putters and I expected that it would keep the batters from stepping out of it. They almost broke a leg stepping on it. Then I used a simple chalk line boundary painted on a mat. That didn't stop them.

"I once took a rubber exerciser that body-builders use to stretch for muscle development. I strapped one end to each foot, figuring that a batter could stretch it only so far while taking a stride. That one almost had 'em killed."

TV: Give Pause to a Whole New Ball Game

In the early fifties, organized baseball experienced a decline in the minor leagues. The decline was largely attributed to unrestricted television broadcasts of major-league games in minor-league territories. Branch Rickey led a fight in Congress for a bill that would give baseball owners the sole right to regulate these broadcasts. The Mahatma's thoughts:

Radio has made major-league fans out of minor-league fans. It created a desire to see something. Television is giving it to them. Once a television set has broken them of the ball-park habit, a great many fans will never reacquire it. And if television makes new baseball customers, as some are claiming, why don't Broadway productions televise their shows? The only way you can see a Broadway production is to buy a ticket—and I cannot concede that baseball has, under the oft-used heading of the "public interest," any obligation to give away continuously at only a fraction of its real worth the only thing it has to sell.

Baseball, properly and legally, can and should control its activities in the field of telecasting.

Telecasting should be confined to stations located within a club's so-called "home territory." Further, I believe that the telecasting of ALL home games, even if confined to one's home territory, is economically unsound. However, each club should be given the right to determine which of its games are telecast.

All members of a league should participate in the receipts of all games telecast. If it should become advisable in the interests of baseball generally that there should be network telecasting of a major-league "game of the day" once a week throughout the country, for example, then the receipts from such a telecasting program should be channeled to the minor leagues for promotional purposes.

We have to be careful about television because the tail could wag the dog.

Knot Hole Gang

In my early years as general manager of the Brooklyn Dodgers, I believed one of the best ways to build our fan base was to establish a "Knot Hole Gang" for youngsters by which they could come into Ebbets Field free of charge and watch a game. I am talking about kids who are in the 12–16-year-old range and who have gained an affection for the game and its stars, and to whom watching them play is truly a memorable occasion.

When we first tried this idea in St. Louis in 1917, we had as many as 10,000 boys and 5,000 girls at a single game. These clubs—whether called Knot Hole Gang, Girls Clubs, or what-not—are not merely means by which boys and girls can see ball games for free. The Knot Hole Gang movement can influence the molding of the character of youngsters. The character-building activities which impose definite responsibilities upon the youngsters are apparent—not to miss school, not to attend a game without their parents' consent, not to use profane language. And, of course, the formation of these organizations places a great responsibility upon professional baseball. It means that the conduct of the game must be exemplary. Baseball must present a solid front of integrity and avoid all that is tawdry and cheapening. We must see that the game dramatizes only such values as sportsmanship, a sense of fair play, and teamwork and cooperation. A great factor in carrying America forward is the teamwork developed on our athletic fields. Athletics are a major influence in a youngster's life. Sports can do more to keep good youngsters good and to make bad youngsters good than all the police forces in the world. The idle youngster is potentially the most vicious agency in a community's life. Sport utilizes the abundant energies of boyhood and directs them into constructive channels. It provides an outlet for the competitive spirit. Wasn't it [the philosopher William] James who said that sport offered the moral equivalent of war? I think it can become that, and as such it should be a major activity in every nation.

CHAPTER SIX

Here's to You, Jackie Robinson

*I*n Rickey's time, the idea that African-Americans belonged in major-
league baseball was not new, just not popular. In his efforts to break
the color barrier, Rickey was honoring two of the principles that
guided his life: provide equality for all and speak out for what is right.
Although his signing of Jackie Robinson was a business decision (to tap a
great pool of talent), its roots sprung from the need to right a wrong.
Read the words of Rickey, Robinson, and others about this pivotal time.

"I think I am the right man to pick for the test. There is no possible
chance that I will flunk it or quit before the end for any other reason than
that I am not a good enough ballplayer."

—Jackie Robinson

The roots of Rickey's campaign to overturn major-league baseball's ban on black players can be traced all the way back to his childhood.

Wesley Branch Rickey was born in 1881, the second son of a small town farm family in south-central Ohio. The Rickeys were devoutly religious Methodists who adhered to the Wesleyan tradition of social liberalism. Self-discipline, education, and hard work were the predominant values in the Rickey home; corporal punishment and alcohol were taboo. The whole family, particularly Branch and his father, Frank, took great delight in discussing and disputing religious principles among themselves and with friends and neighbors.

By the time Branch headed off to Ohio Wesleyan University in the Spring of 1901, his core social and moral belief was that all men and women are indeed created equal.

◇

In April of the 1904 season, the Ohio Wesleyan baseball team, coached by Branch Rickey, was slated to play Notre Dame, in South Bend, Indiana. When Rickey and his players entered the lobby of the Oliver Hotel to register, the clerk informed Rickey that Charles Thomas, the team's only African American, would not be given a room.

Rickey turned to the team's student manager and asked him to go to the local YMCA to try to get a room, not only for Thomas but for the rest of the team as well. Rickey then asked to speak to the hotel manager. After a long, private conference in the manager's office, Rickey marched Tommy toward Rickey's room, where Thomas would wait until lodging could be found for him in South Bend's black neighborhood. On the way, Rickey said to Barney Russell, the team manager, under his breath: "Forget about the YMCA. Tommy stays with us."

When they arrived at the room, Rickey called the front desk to order a cot. The angry hotel manager told Rickey that he had broken his word. The even angrier Rickey bellowed: "Under no circumstances will I leave or allow Thomas to be put out!"

"We went upstairs," Rickey recalled years later. "I summoned the team captain to discuss plans for the game. Tommy stood in the corner, tense and brooding and in silence. I asked him to sit in a chair and relax. Instead, he sat on the end of the cot, his huge shoulders hunched and his large hands clasped between his knees. I tried to talk to our captain, but I couldn't take my gaze from Tommy. Tears welled in his eyes. They spilled down his face. Then his shoulders heaved convulsively, and he rubbed one great hand over the other with all the power of his body, muttering, 'Black skin, black skin. If I could only make 'em white.' He kept rubbing and rubbing as though he would remove the blackness by sheer friction.

"'C'mon, Tommy! If you can't lick it, how can you expect us to help? Buck up.'" Charles Thomas did buck up. He played in the Notre Dame game and remained on the team throughout the season.

Decades later, as he was preparing to orchestrate Jackie Robinson's entry in to the major leagues, Rickey described the effect of Charles Thomas's ordeal in South Bend on his own life:

"Whatever mark that incident left on the Charles Thomas, it was no more indelible than the impressions made on me.

In 1958, Thomas, who had become a dentist in Albuquerque, New Mexico, recalled his college experience:

"From the first day I entered OWU, Rickey took a special interest in my welfare. I think I was the first Negro player on its teams, and some fellows didn't welcome me any too kindly, but there was no open opposition.

"I always felt that Branch set them straight. During the three years that I was at OWU, no man could have treated me better. When we went on our trips, Rickey was the first one to see if I was welcome in the hotel where we were to stop. On several occasions, he talked the manager into letting me occupy a double room with him and his roommate, Barney Russell."

How can you call it an All-American sport if you exclude black Americans?

—Arthur Mann, Rickey biographer

Since the late 1880s, the owners of major-league teams had operated under a "gentlemen's agreement," whereby they would not employ Negro players. Rickey was determined to put an end to this policy. The very first thing I did when I came to Brooklyn in late 1942 was to investigate the approval of ownership for a Negro player. There was timeliness about the notion. The Negro in America was legally but never morally free. I thought: If the right man with control of himself could be found . . .

I spent $25,000 in all the Caribbean countries . . . Puerto Rico, Cuba, employed two scouts, one for an entire year in Mexico, only to find that the greatest Negro players were in our own country. *By early 1945, Rickey's scouts had determined that at least eight were of major-league caliber: catchers Josh Gibson and Roy Campanella, first baseman Buck Leonard, second baseman Marvin William, shortstops Jackie Robinson and Piper Davis, and outfielders Cool Papa Bell and Sam Jethroe.*

Not Just a Great Player, But a Model Citizen

Rickey once explained why he needed to find not just a great player, but a model citizen: I had to get the right man, off the field. I couldn't come with a man to break down a tradition that had centered and concentrated all the prejudices of a great many people, north and south, unless he was good. He must justify himself on the principle of merit. He must be a great player; I must not risk an excuse of trying to do something in the sociological field, or in the race field, just because of a sort of "holier than thou." I must be sure that the man was good on the field, but more dangerous to me, at that time and even now, was the wrong man off the field. It didn't matter to me so much in choosing a man off the field that he was temperamental—righteously subject to resentments. I wanted a man of exceptional intelligence, a man who was able to grasp and control the responsibilities of himself to his race and could carry that load. That was the greatest danger point of all.

By the beginning of the 1945 season, Rickey and his scouts has narrowed the choice to Jackie Robinson. On August 18, 1945, Jackie Robinson and Branch Rickey met face to face. During the meeting, which lasted three hours, Rickey alternately chastised and cajoled, threatened and reassured. At one point, Rickey read to Robinson from Giovanni Papini's The Life of Christ:

> *"Ye have heard that it hath been said, An eye for an eye and a tooth for a tooth: But I say unto you that ye resist not evil: But whosoever shall smite thee on the right cheek, turn to him the other . . . There are three answers men can make to violence: revenge, flight, turning the other cheek. The first is the barbarous principle of retaliation. Flight is no better than retaliation. The man who takes flight invites pursuit. Turning the other cheek means not receiving the second blow. It means cutting the chains of the inevitable wrongs at the first link. Your adversary is ready for anything but this . . . Every man has an obscure respect for courage in others, especially if it is moral courage, the rarest and most difficult sort of bravery. It makes the very brute understand that this man is more than a man. The results of nonresistance, even if they are not always perfect, are certainly superior to resistance or flight. To answer blows with blows, evil deeds with evil deeds, is to meet the attacker on his own ground, to proclaim oneself as low as he. Only he who has conquered himself can conquer his enemies."*

When he finished reading the passage, Rickey turned to Robinson and asked: "Now, can you do it? I know you are naturally combative. But for three years—three years—you will have to do it the only way it can be done. Three years—can you do it?"

"What will you do," Rickey shouted, *"what will you do when they call you a black son of a bitch? When they not only turn you down for a hotel room but also curse you out?"* Rickey was on his feet—pacing and sweating. He sat down then quickly got up again and went over to Robinson. Robinson was tense, his fists clenched. Suddenly Rickey threw his own fist into Robinson's face, *"WHAT DO YOU DO?"* he screamed.

Robinson whispered, *"Mr. Rickey, I've got two cheeks. If you want to take this gamble, I'll promise you there will be no incidents."*

I know I am heading for trouble in Florida next month when I must train with Montreal. I don't look for anything physical. I really believe we've gotten beyond that in this country. I know I'll take a tongue beating though, but I think I can take it. I'm due for a terrible riding from the bench jockeys all around the International League circuit if I am good enough to play with Montreal all summer. I know about the riding the white players give one another, and I'm sure it will be much worse for me because I am a Negro. They'll try to upset me and they'll have plenty of material, but we've got that also in our league and I am prepared for it. These days keep reminding me of something my mother told me when I was a little kid. She told me that the words they say about you can't hurt you. And when they see that, they'll quit saying them. I've had plenty of nasty things said about me from the stands, especially in basketball, where you can hear everything they shout. I never let it get to me. I think it made me play better. I'll always remember what my mother taught me, and I think I'll come through.

—*Jackie Robinson (1946)*

When the announcement had been made that Jackie Robinson would join the Montreal club for the 1946 season, Branch Rickey was accused in a Look *magazine article of excessive moralizing. Rickey promptly called a*

press conference. In the following excerpts from that conference, Rickey reveals his personal convictions and the subtle diplomacy he had practiced as pilot of the Robinson mission:

There's a current magazine, which is now on the newsstand, called *Look*, and there's a story in it. I haven't read it, can't even tell you the title, but it has a picture of me there in a perplexed state of mind, apparently. I don't know if the photograph printed there is intended to indicate supplication before our Father-in-Heaven, whether it is a state of good resignation to a condition that I can't avoid or help. I don't know whether it's intended with the words accompanying the picture to indicate that I wish to defend myself against a move I have made in regard to the colored baseball player in this country.

Perhaps it's intended to indicate an admission that on social grounds or economic grounds it cannot be defended and that I seek the moral atmosphere—that I am saying that, like a publican on the street corner with a holier-than-thou toga about me, "Oh, Lord, I can't face you any longer without recognizing the colored ballplayer in this country." That seems to be the indication of the picture. I never considered that God Almighty was too concerned with what I regarded as in incipient duty of mankind to one another.

Print that. I had rather that they had printed that instead of what they have me saying in a quote on that page. I never said it. If it has implications of holiness about it—you boys know me—I have had a personal background that has sort of put me on a pedestal: he's a goody-goody fellow, he's a pin-cushion moralist, he's a softy. Well, maybe so, a man can't estimate himself like other people can judge him to be in character. If there are some of the habiliments of hypocrisy that you can't remove, the best thing is not to talk about them—live your life as best you can. Do the best you can.

This thing I have done was a thing I felt I had to do. I could not do otherwise, and I doubt if there is a single man in this room who, had he been sitting beside me from one step to the other from the beginning to now would do one thing differently than has been done by the Brooklyn baseball club. I very much doubt it. I think you would have done exactly what has been done.

I mentioned something [about morality] in order to remove it out of the many causes for what I did. I mentioned it because I don't want it to linger in your mind as the reason why I did it.

I can't tell the difference between dark skin and light skin. I'm interested enough to know the likes and dislikes of men, but it never occurred to me that it was necessary to select a team because of race, creed, or color. I'll go down on that. I'm out to win a pennant. If this fellow can help me more to win the pennant as a team fact, I'm going to employ him. And I did. I don't know if this fellow can make this ball club. Know if he does make the Montreal baseball club, he won't be given any favors, because he's just another American citizen. Pretty good sort of chap maybe, and that's all; that's it. It's the inevitable, not a move; it's a movement.

Rickey believed that close interaction could help in tearing down the walls of prejudice. (1946)

Clay Hopper, Jackie's first manager, took me by the lapels of my coat as he sat there sweating in his underclothes watching a game over on the inside park at Daytona Beach. This boy [Robinson] had made a great play in the fourth inning and I had remarked about it. In the seventh inning, Jackie made one of those tremendous and remarkable plays that very few people can make—went toward first base, made a slide, stabbed the ball, came up with it in his left hand glove, and turned with body control that's almost inconceivable and cut off the runner at second base on a force play. I took Clay and I put my hand on his shoulder and I said, "Did you ever see a play to beat it?"

Now this fellow comes from Greenwood, Mississippi. And he took me and shook me and his face that far from 'em and he said, "Do you really think that a nigger is a human being Mr. Rickey?" That's what he said. That's what this fellow said. I never answered him.

Six months later he came into my office after the year in Montreal when he was this boy's manager. He hadn't wanted Robinson to be sent to him. And he said to me, "I want to take back what I said to you last spring." He said, "I'm ashamed of it. Now, do you have plans for him to be on your club? If you don't have plans to have him on the Brooklyn club, I would like to have him back at Montreal. He was not only a great ballplayer, good enough for Brooklyn, but also a fine gentleman."

In the summer of 1946, the major-league owners were well aware that Jackie Robinson was playing for the Dodgers' farm team in Montreal and that he was poised to be promoted to the Brooklyn club the next spring. Still determined to keep blacks out of baseball, they issued a formal report on August 27, 1946, which claimed that the integration of the major leagues would be harmful to Negro players and would bring about the ruination of the Negro Leagues.

Before they commissioned the report, the owners voted 15-1 to retain the gentlemen's agreement that had kept blacks out of the game for sixty years. The sole dissenting vote was cast by the Dodgers. Furious at the owners' behavior, Rickey visited the one person who might help—Happy Chandler. As commissioner of the major leagues, Chandler had the power to overrule the owners in any matter he deemed contrary to "the best interests of baseball." The question was whether the affable Chandler would be willing to defy the wishes of 15 of the 16 clubs over an issue that, at the least, had the potential to disrupt the national pastime and, at the worst, to enflame race relations in the country.

Rickey flew to Chandler's home in Kentucky to discuss the matter. The two gentlemen talked and dined together for several hours, looking at every side of the Robinson issue. After dinner they retired to Chandler's den where, according to the commissioner, they had the following exchange:

Rickey said, "I can't go ahead in the face of that vote. I can't do it unless I'm assured of your support."

"Can this man play?"

"He could make the major leagues today," said Rickey.

"Then the only reason he's being kept out is because he's black," Chandler concluded. "Let's bring him in and treat him as just another player. I'll keep an eye on him."

With this simple, pivotal action, Chandler pushed the baseball owners aside and cleared the way for Jackie Robinson to step up to the major-league plate.

I was told that a Negro had signed to play for Brooklyn, although I'd have to say that the word that was used was not "Negro." Like most Americans who were white, I didn't know what a Negro athlete was like. I just assumed they weren't good enough for the big leagues. I had heard the talk, you know, that if you threw at them, they backed down. On learning Jackie Robinson was a shortstop: Dammit, I thought, there are nine positions on the field and this guy has got to be a shortstop like me. I began to wonder what the people in Louisville would think about me playing with a colored boy. Then I thought, the hell with anyone who didn't like it. He deserved a chance just like everybody else.

—PeeWee Reese

When Robinson arrived for spring training in 1947, the one remaining concern was whether his major-league teammates would accept him. Rickey was certain of only one thing: Dodger manager Leo Durocher would be a source of support.

A few days after the team's arrival in Panama for its first exhibition game, several veteran players were drawing up a petition demanding Robinson's removal. Before the petition could be presented, however, Durocher *called the would-be signers into his office in the middle of the night and laid down the law: "You know what you can do with that petition. You can wipe your ass with it. Mr. Rickey is on his way down here, and all you have to do is tell him about it."*

"I'll play an elephant if he can do the job," Durocher continued, "This fellow is a real great ballplayer. He's going to win a pennant for us. From everything I hear, he's only the first. Only the first, boys!" Later that morning, Rickey spoke to the malcontents individually. Most of them withdrew their complaints although a few stood firm. Several weeks later, Rickey commented: "First they'll endure Robinson, then pity him, then embrace him."

You'd hear a lot of insults from the opposing benches during games, guys calling him things like "nigger" and "watermelon eater," trying to rile him. But that was when Jackie Robinson started to turn the tables. You saw how he stood there at the plate and dared them to hit him with the ball, and you began to put yourself in his shoes. You'd think of yourself trying to break into the black leagues, maybe, and what it would be like—and I know that I couldn't have done it. In a word, he was winning respect.

—PeeWee Reese (1947)

After a series with the Philadelphia Phillies in 1947 marked by persistent racial abuse on the part of the Phillies' bench, Rickey had this observation: "The Chapman incident [Phillies' manager Ben Chapman led the abuse] did more than anything to make the Dodgers speak up on Robinson's behalf. When Chapman and the others poured out that string of unconscionable abuse, he solidified and unified thirty men, not one of whom was willing to see someone kick around a man who had his hands tied behind his back. Chapman created in Robinson's behalf a thing called sympathy, the most unifying word in the world.

That word has a Greek origin—it means "to suffer." To say, "I sympathize with you" is to say, "I suffer with you." That is what Chapman
did. He caused men like Stanky to suffer with Robinson, and he made
this Negro a real member of the Dodgers.

I realized the point would come when my almost filial relationship
with Jackie would break with ill feeling if I did not issue an emanci-
pation proclamation for him. I could see how the tensions had built
up in him for two years and that this young man had come through
with courage far beyond what I had asked; yet, I knew that burning
inside him was the same pride and determination that burned inside
those Negro slaves a century earlier. I knew also that while the wisest
policy for Robinson during those first two years was to turn the other
cheek and not fight back, there were many in baseball who would not
understand his lack of action. They could be made to respect courage
only in the physical sense. So I told Robinson that he was on his own.
Then I sat back happily, knowing that, with the restraints removed,
Robinson was going to show the National League a thing or two.

*Looking back, I can see how the conviction of Jackie and Mr. Rickey to
bring a black into baseball was fortified by the fact that they were alike in
so many ways. Jackie had the good influence of older men in his life, and
he was deeply spiritual, with a strong belief in God. Both were religious,
and both said "we" rather than "I." We could always call Mr. Rickey on
the phone; he was always available to us. It wasn't as if he had just thrust
Jack into a situation and left him to fend for himself, he took responsibility.*

*Nor were we ever distrustful of Mr. Rickey's motives. He was a man
of integrity, and we could trust him. Whatever his mixed motives may have
been, he became a lifelong friend, someone we admired tremendously.*

—Rachel Robinson, wife of Jackie

Before Branch Rickey moved to Pittsburgh, in 1950, where Branch later became general manager of the Pirates, Jackie Robinson wrote this letter to his former mentor:

"I have been intending to write for a month now, and it seems that finding the right words comes hard, so I will attempt at this time to put them down.

"It is certainly tough on everyone in Brooklyn to have you leave the organization, but to me it's much worse, and I don't mind saying we (my family) hate to see you go but realize baseball is like that and anything can happen. It has been the finest experience I have had being associated with you, and I want to thank you very much for all you have meant, not only to me and my family but to the entire country and particularly the members of our race. I am glad for your sake that I had a small part to do with the success of your efforts, and I must admit it was your constant guidance that enabled me to do so. Regardless of what happens to me in the future, it can all be placed on what you have done, and believe me, I appreciate it. I hope to end my playing days in Brooklyn, as it means so very much, but if I have to go any place, I hope it can be with you.

"My wife joins me in saying thank you very much, Mr. Rickey. And we sincerely hope that we can always be regarded as your friends and whenever we need advice we can call on you as usual, regardless of where we may be.

"My very best wishes to you and yours and a hope for your continued success."

A Moderate Is a Moral Pickpocket

Ninety-five years ago, we told three-and-one-half-million Negro slaves that they were free. Free for what? Free from what? Free to do what? We didn't say that at first. Then we passed the 14th and 15th Amendments trying to identify and describe freedom. And now here they are, no longer in chains, but often and in many areas with no more sense of real freedom than they had a century ago. Sure, they can travel. "I can go to New York or Chicago and nobody can stop me," says the Negro. And what then? Let us not be surprised if seventeen million Negroes now organize to win a fair representation in government. Why shouldn't they identify with any party organization that promises them freedom from discrimination everywhere? And once the Negroes organize effectively in certain areas in this country, we must be prepared to see political control pass locally to colored citizens. If that day comes, it would be too much to expect all Negroes to forgive and to forget the record of the past one hundred years. I am afraid the white man will justly reap as he has sown.

How long will the white citizens of this country go on ignoring the agony of the Negro? How long will he be tempted to look elsewhere for equal rights—not only civil, political, and educational rights—but just simple human rights?

They call you an extremist if you want integration now—which is the only morally defensible position. To advise moderation is like going to a stickup man and saying to him: "Don't use a gun. That's violent. Why not be a pickpocket instead?" A moderate is a moral pickpocket. *(1956)*

CHAPTER SEVEN

For the Record

T his section offers Rickey's musings on varied subjects: family, definition of success, money, aging, alcohol, and his all-time, all-star team:

While managing the St. Louis Browns at the tail end of their 1914 season, Rickey was coaxed into taking one more major-league at-bat. Rickey stepped to the plate on condition that Athletics pitcher Ray Bressler not throw any curves. I was sure they'd curve me to death, so I wasn't set for the first pitch, strike one, fastball. Well, I thought, that was done to make me complacent. I just knew they'd bend the next one over.

The next pitch was a fastball, a strike. I was now ready for the curve and was utterly astonished to see a third fastball go by—strike three. My last turn at bat in the major leagues taught me that nothing is gained by distrusting your fellow man.

Words to Live By

Ol' man opportunity has long hair in front and he is bald behind. When he comes to you, you can snatch him and hold him tight, but when he is past, he could be gone forever.

Things don't happen without a cause. They just don't. There's a reason for pretty nearly everything that happens that I know about.

Intuition is our subconscious reaction in times of stress.

My father was 86 when he died. As an old man, he was still planting peach and apple trees on our farm. When I asked him who would take care of the fruit, he said, "That's not important. I just want to live every day as if I were going to live forever."

Never surrender opportunity for security.

I don't like any "ism" whose existence depends upon force.

There is a disturbing extracurricular activity furnished by the "party man"—usually the victim of local hero worshippers who invite him, e.g., out to dinner. The cocktail, which should be no part of the major-leaguer's diet, may be the start of ultimate trouble. I've seen the mixture of alcohol and professional baseball for 60 years. They don't mix to the advantage of the player. Total abstinence is the only sensible safeguard for the player.

I don't like silent men when personal liberty is at stake.

Up Close and Personal

I just can't slow down. I'd rather die ten minutes sooner than be doing nothing all the time. But I do hope that on some distant day in the future my funeral cortege will move at a leisurely pace.

I earned my living when I was eighteen teaching in a country school in Ohio. It was a feuding district, with a moonshiner right up the holler. Five of my pupils were older than I was, and at the end of the day I'd have to scrub the tobacco juice off my shoes!

Branch Rickey's three "abides": I had five daughters and a son. There was a time when I was having trouble figuring out their lifestyles, particularly my second daughter, a flaxen-haired beauty who had a taste for young men that ran totally counter to what I thought was proper.

We parried back and forth for nearly a year on the subject as it related to a particular young man she was seeing. It finally reached a point where I had to declare the qualities I believed were most important. We had a discussion one Saturday night after a family dinner.

I called them the three "abides." And I gave the subject considerable thought before laying it out.

The first is honesty. Honesty is a relative thing. Even the person that's just on the threshhold of Heaven, and has never had an act or thought in his life that wouldn't approach perfection, probably couldn't justify the position that a lie is never justifiable. Of course, there are exceptions, such as not telling a dying person the nature of their malady and its inevitable outcome to help make their final days as mentally comfortable as possible.

My meaning of honesty is that it holds the respect of other people, that there would be no doubt about the integrity and action of a man who's honest. Such a man wouldn't withhold any fact which was entitled to be known in the making of a deal. He would not be subject to the charge of guilty concealment. He told it all. He would lay it all on the table as it is pertinent to the case. Then he will, of course, not deliberately assert something to be true that is not true.

The second attribute, I told my family, is industriousness.

"What's that got to do with it?" my fourth daughter asked.

I said it means putting a shelter over her head. It means clothing to put on. It means food to sustain her. It means effort to do it. If there is failure to provide the necessities, there is complete embracing of the effort on the part of my daughter. She will sympathize with him. She will understand the futility, the failure of his efforts. She'll share them, and in that is found happiness. He doesn't necessarily have to have money or health. He can lose both.

And the third is infinite kindness—a kindness that transcends the forms of courtesy. Just the little things: opening the door for her, to guide her over an icy sidewalk so she doesn't fall; carefully observing the amenities so they will be followed; the formalities of recognition of the sex as worthy of care because they are not as strong physically as the husband. Infinite kindness will sustain a marriage through all its problems, its uncertainties, its illnesses, its disappointments, its storms, its tensions, its fear, its separations, its sorrows. Out of infinite kindness grow real love and understanding and tolerance and warmth. Nothing can take the place of such an enduring asset.

I find fault with my children because I like them and I want them to go places. When they don't show the signs of going places—uprightness and strength and courage and civic respect and anything that affects the probabilities of failure on the part of those that are closest to me, that concern me—I find fault.

I never did go to high school, and never saw the inside of one until after I went to Delaware. I was a preparatory student with two years of so-called prep work to do in order to become a freshman. I carried as many as twenty-one hours in one term and never did catch up with my classes until the spring term of 1904 . . . I did the preparatory work and four years of college in three-and-a-third years.

On his first season playing with the Cincinnati Reds (1904): I was as green as grass and happy as a kid with his first fish on the line, being out there with the players I'd dreamed about. Heinie [Peitz] was swell, even loaned me his chest protector and mitt since I didn't have any equipment of my own. *Although on the team, Rickey never appeared in a game.*

Rickey always asked his players about their families. When a player said he hoped to have boys, Rickey would tell him: Remember when your children grow up, the daughters always bring their husbands and their children to your home for Christmas. The sons always go to the wives' home.

I do not remember a time that I was ever in rags. That I was poor on a standard of community wealth in that part of the country where I was reared, that would be correct. And if I was rich, ever, that would not be correct either. I struggled all the way along to have a great team and have it on a sportsmanlike basis. Money was useful and I wanted it; I had a numerous family and I wanted them to go to college and I wanted them to have all the opportunities that could properly be afforded to a boy or girl in this country. Those were the objectives, I take it, and I worked for that. I don't think that, all my life put together, I have had five minutes conversation about salary. My compensations, I think, are pretty largely my satisfactions in having a home and family and lovely children and devotion of some friends. Nobody has too many friends, most are a little fairweatherish, but it's a wonderful thing to feel the identification with a great number of groups of boys who work very hard for a common purpose and have some realization of an accomplishment at some time or other. That's been true in all my life.

When I was in Ann Arbor in Law School (*Class of 1911*), I told the girl I married that I thought I would be successful and the day would come that I could have a stenographer. I said, then I will consider myself successful. Well, now, that day came but I felt I was pretty far away from any kind of definition of success. And then I remembered that I substituted another definition for success and that was that I would be able to retire, really, when I was 45 years of age. Well, I got to be 45 years of age and I felt like I had not succeeded by any manner of means and then I adopted another objective. Looking toward this thing which I might call success, I said if ever I get to be the master of my time, then I feel that I will be successful. Well, these things that you call satisfaction, happiness and success, they are by-products, in my judgment. They hang around maybe close to you, but the fun comes out of pursuit, the joy in trying to do a job of some kind.

PROSPECTS AND SUSPECTS **Bill White** ♦ Above average runner. Not a strong arm, but he has a lot of power. He strikes out more than he should, which is not surprising. I believe his bat position gives him a real problem in timing the pitch. But he is hitting with power, and nothing should be said to any batsman who is doing well. Let him alone. However, his stance mystifies me. When the ball leaves the pitcher's hands, Bill's bat is in a positive perpendicular position. His hands are in front of his left shoulder, and, of course, in order to get the power he really has, he must go back with his hands and particularly with the big end of the bat. That doubles his problem in timing, because he is going in two directions. I know of only one or two great batsmen who have what I call this preliminary batting fault. Jackie Robinson had it, but he corrected it largely by pushing his hands out away from his body and placing them well back of his shoulder. And then he got the habit of that position. *(1962) White batted .286 in 13 major-league seasons, but he is more renowned for his work as a broadcaster and president of the National League. White had originally entered college as a medical student, but opted for a career as a ballplayer instead of a doctor.*

I wonder why a man trained for the law devotes his life to something so cosmically unimportant as a game.

She had a beautiful life of toil and love. All the folks in the entire countryside thought she was wonderful—old men and boys, and particularly young women in childbirth and poor folks who were "on the township trust" for food—and the drinking chaps—she took them in too. She has been in my mind all my knowing life and most certainly she is the most unforgettable character I ever knew.

She was my mother.

The Game and Other Cosmic Issues

Football will never replace baseball as our national pastime. It is too rough a contact sport for young limbs—and if you appraise the modern safety equipment, who can afford it?

I had a letter some time ago, from a young chap who said he had been reading Bill Doak's article on how to pitch, and felt that he was qualified now for a trial with the Dodgers. It isn't enough. Men cannot learn to play baseball unless they project themselves contractually into the field of play. Such book-players could quickly join the army of "grand-stand managers," those who can ask plausible but impossible questions and make safe second-guess criticisms. Their preparation is good as far as it goes, but it doesn't go very far.

This is a marvelous business. It really is. It has permanency in it. It has challenge to it. It has great interest in it. It has leisure in it. It has compensation in it. And in several fields, the longer your whiskers grow in this game, the better qualified you are to serve it.

Baseball, insofar as big business goes, is a comparatively small industry. *The World Almanac* (1946), just off the press, lists 43 billion-dollar companies in the United States. The minimum salary paid a major-league player (for six months' actual work) is higher than the average salary paid the employees of any one of these 43 great organizations. Yet the profit return on dollar investment in baseball is less than the profit return on dollar investment in 28 of these billion-dollar organizations on which figures were available. Surely that record cannot be called selfish.

Charges are made that baseball owners exploit their players. True enough, baseball is a competitive business, and in order to maintain competition it is necessary to operate under certain rules of contract reserve that do not exist in other forms of industry. The player, because he is in a competitive business, has a shorter professional career than men in other industries.

These facts we recognize. The two major leagues have entered into an agreement whereby within the next ten years a cash fund totaling $5 million will be set up from baseball's *own* funds—not for purpose of development, but to pay "back-service" pension rights for players now in the twilight of their major-league careers and establish a pension plan that will provide a life income to a player who serves in the majors as little as five years—with the "selfish" owners themselves contributing 80% of the monies necessary to make that pension available. Would you classify that action as extreme selfishness and exploitation?

These are uncertain times. We cannot be content to rest on yesterday's laurels. These are times when we must strengthen rather than let down those standards which have stood in such good stead in crises that are past. Baseball cannot be selfish, or irresponsible, or lax. Neither can the men who operate it.

My years in Brooklyn (1943–50) gave me a new vision of America, or rather America gave me a new vision of a part of itself, Brooklyn. They were wonderful years. A community of over three million people, proud, hurt, jealous, seeking geographical, social, emotional status as a city apart and alone and sufficient. One could not live for eight years in Brooklyn and not catch its spirit of devotion to its baseball club, such as no other city in America equalled. Call it loyalty and so it was. It was a crime against a community of three million people to move the Dodgers. Not that the move was unlawful, since people have a right to do as they please with their property. But a baseball club in any city in America is a quasi-public institution, and in Brooklyn the Dodgers were public without the quasi. Not even a succeeding generation could forget or forgive the removal of the Dodgers to California. Oh, my, what a team they were!

The game invades our language! Now, the editorial page of the *New York Times* is a serious forum, not ordinarily given to levity. Yet at the height of the controversy between the Army and Senator McCarthy, there was the line on this dignified editorial page, "Senator McCarthy—a good fastball, but no control." Now, didn't that tell the whole story in a sentence?

Mr. Rickey's Lexicon:
- *Dead Body—player with poor reflexes and timing.*
- *Pantywaist—player who is a non-winner, a follower.*
- *Captain—take charge player.*
- *Corporals—players on Rickey's team with a limited future.*
- *Privates—players that lacked any future in baseball.*

The game of baseball has given me a life of joy. I would not have exchanged it for any other.

Cream of the Crop

Hung on Rickey's office walls were photographs of athletes he admired most: Honus Wagner, George Sisler, Rogers Hornsby, Charlie Barrett, Leo Durocher, and Jackie Robinson.

Ted Williams would sit on the second step of the Red Sox dugout with his cap off and sun himself and study the hitters in the cage. He would learn something about hitting every day and help the young hitters on the other team right behind the cage if they asked his advice. When he stepped in the batting cage he cared for only one thing; to hit! How can a man with eyes like that not be a great hitter? His exceptional vision triggered his gargantuan swing.

Stan Musial was the most-liked player in the league. He would hit everywhere, but in Ebbets Field he would hit especially well. It was said that Musial owned Ebbets Field. When he coiled for the pitcher's delivery with Roy Campanella behind the plate for Brooklyn and then stepped into a pitch, it was a double in the alley or a quick goodbye over the wire-screen fence into Bedford Avenue. The faithful in Flatbush will always remember him at that moment.

I never did see Dizzy Dean feeling right on a day he was supposed to pitch. He loved to be babied and cajoled and wheedled. I remember one day a very important game with the Pirates was coming up. Dizzy put on a long moan to me that afternoon, saying he could not possibly pitch. Said his arm ached like all get-out.

I thought fast and remembered that the Mayor was coming out to the game that day. I'd given him a few box seats. So I said to Diz: Too bad, now I'll have to tell the Major not to come. He was coming out to see you pitch. But now. . . ." "Wait a minute," said Dizzy, "maybe I could make it. I'll try hard to pitch for your sake, Mr. Rickey." You see, he loved to perform, loved to be in the spotlight. So I said to him: "Well, Dizzy, give it a try. Warm up, and if you pitch only one ball in the game and then retire that'll leave me all right with the Mayor." Well Dizzy did a piece of pitching that afternoon. Gave 'em three hits, fanned about a dozen, and they haven't got a run off him yet!

Terry Moore was a real Gashouser. In him burned the fire and determination of a crusader. A warrior. He asked no quarter and gave none.

Honus Wagner lived the game, slept and ate only to play. No name has ever been mentioned to compare with his versatility, his ability to play all positions. He could make my all-time baseball team at any position, but most would place him at shortstop. When Wagner scooped up a ground ball on a dusty field, the first fifteen feet in the fast flight of the ball was sometimes dust cloud. One first baseman said that he simply picked out the biggest object from the cloud and caught it. It was usually the ball. His only upset, visible to others, was his reaction to a wrong call by the umpire, and it had to be **wrong, very wrong,** for you to find it out from Honus.

The man who evidenced the greatest degree of physical courage that I ever knew in the game of baseball was Cobb. He didn't really have more courage, if there were ways to measure it, in the field of moral standards or physical standards; he probably had no more than a great many men I could name. But he had that carelessness about showmanship; such utter disregard of the sportive rights of competitors that he violated them and let the chips fall where they would and he had deservedly the reputation of being a very aggressive player. Courage, yes. Guts, they call it. Yes. Of course he was unafraid. But he had superlative skills and ability with it and they enabled him to do things that others didn't and couldn't do. Skill puts the chrome on courage.

Babe Ruth is known chiefly as a home-run hitter. He was very much more than that. He could run and field, both above average, and had an extraordinarily strong arm. He could play any position. But his physical prowess dominated and led to practically every distinction that came to him. He had a bodily capacity for life's selectives faster and fuller than most. He could not live a single minute simply as a breathing person. His physiological appetites sought instant, persistent, and enduring satisfaction. His was the life of pursuit—vibrant joy in the chase. He never gave thought to tomorrow. He lived for today, now—for the very next stroke of the bat. Wherever he might be or whatever he might be doing, he could always become very quickly "as a little child." I can think of Babe Ruth entering Heaven upon that simple Biblical requirement.

Christy Mathewson was a perfectionist in the art of pitching. Any professional pitcher can produce many different directions of the rotation or spin of the ball. Not many have much selectivity, or any at all, in changing the rapidity of the rotation other than the knuckle ball. Mathewson was a master of both. His manager, John McGraw, once said, "When a hit meant a run, or the game, he was as close to being invincible as any pitcher." He was skilled in games that required memory, such as checkers, chess, whist, and later, bridge. My own skill at checkers is "country good." I learned from unsympathetic cracker-barrel experts. Yet, I could never win a game from Matty.

I challenge any baseball man to observe Willie Mays in uniform on offense and defense for 7,200 consecutive seconds and, with a clear conscience, not include mention of him on the All-Time Team. This fellow plays the game all the time. His hitting, fielding, throwing, running, discipline, health, agility, and desire rate him with the best. In modern baseball, Mays is in a class by himself. *Rickey chose Ty Cobb as his all-time centerfielder.*

On the Gashouse Gang: It was a high class team, with nine heavy drinkers who were paid more money over a period of ten years than any other club in the National League, excluding their World Series takes. They were the best team I ever had.

After Roy Campanella's accident (1958), which left him paralyzed in a wheelchair: Don't do what some ballplayers do, Campy. Never give it less than what they ask. Continue to do more, and I know that when I see you next time, I'll bet you a quarter that you'll be able to grab my hand instead of my having to reach for yours.

Just for Fun

On his bow ties: It's cheaper than a regular tie, and it takes less time to put on. It could also cover up a soiled shirt or frayed collar.

It's too bad that in our economic system we have to regulate our lives with a time clock. There would have been too much monotony for me all these years if I had to work in a job starting at 9 A.M. and quitting at 5 P.M. I would have looked forward to retirement. I want to die working. *A reflection on his 71st birthday.*

At the age of 82, Rickey was asked what his greatest thrill in baseball was. "Son, it hasn't happened yet."

Branch Rickey heading toward 83: People complain about the weather. It couldn't be more trivial. Any weather is good enough, as long as you're around to feel it.

When asked if he would have any influence in the selection of a coach by Dodger manager Leo Durocher: Generally speaking, no. But I might. And could and should perhaps. In a given case that is.

I completed college in three years. I was in the top ten percent of my class in law school. I'm a Doctor of Jurisprudence. I am an honorary Doctor of Law. Tell me why I spent four mortal hours today conversing with a person named Dizzy Dean.

Branch Rickey describing Leo Durocher: He has the most fertile talent in the world for making a bad situation infinitely worse.

Worry is simply thinking the same thing over and over again, thinking in cycles and not doing anything about it.

My advice to the young player is not to show an early greed. Allow your salary to follow your ability. You'll be happier, enjoy a longer career, acquire more friends, and make more money.

BRANCH RICKEY'S ALL-TIME TEAM

Position	Best Players Seen	Career Average	His Best Players	Career Average
1B	George Sisler	.340	George Sisler	.340
2B	Eddie Collins	.333	Rogers Hornsby	.358
SS	Honus Wagner	.329	Bobby Wallace	.267
3B	Rogers Hornsby	.358	Frank Frisch	.316
LF	Ed Delahanty	.346	Chick Hafey	.319
CF	Ty Cobb	.367	Duke Snider	.306
RF	Babe Ruth	.342	Terry Moore	.282
C	Roger Bresnahan	.279	Bill DeLancey	.291
P	Walter Johnson	(414-280)	Dizzy Dean	(150-83)

CHAPTER EIGHT

The Deacon

*S*pirituality was an essential part of Rickey's life. It lifted a man up, showed him the way, and kept him from the wrong path. He saw the good of religion everywhere and speaks of its benefits in this chapter.

A Driving Spiritual Force

Of course, there are fundamental physical qualifications for all positions. For most of them, a player must have a good throwing arm, fleetness of foot, and hitting power. For pitching, we look for a loose, well-coordinated delivery, and the ability—in the vernacular of the game—to "throw a high, hard one." In other words, a good fastball. But over and above these basic qualities, there is a great common denominator for all positions: a driving spiritual force that puts a man over, whether he's an athlete or not.

I believe that a man can play baseball as coming to him from a call from God.

Ballplayers, when they acquire big names and fancy salaries, hate to make public appearances. Don't you be like that. Make them, and don't be a snob about it. Be a part of your community life. Give something of yourself.

Don't you tell me that physical intercourse is necessary to a young man. One of the greatest players I ever had in the World Series—he never had contact with any woman—he never had physical intercourse with any woman until he was 28 years of age, and then he married a schoolteacher out in the Middle West.

A white lie is justifiable when the answer will be harmful and when the person seeking the answer is not entitled to ask the question.

A person can be so sincere about rules and law as to blind himself to justice.

I don't like the subtle insinuating infiltration of "something for nothing" philosophies into the very hearthstone of the American family. I believe that "Thou shalt earn bread by the sweat of thy face," was a benediction and not a penalty. I believe that thrift is and should be a blessing to mankind. Work is the zest of life—there is joy in pursuit.

There is something basic that carries a man through all his difficulties if he has a positive religious experience—all his own. He could come in at 4:00 A.M. in violation of every rule, and the manager would not be too concerned to inquire about his whereabouts. Such an experience may be different with other men, depending upon their own faith, but it has to have some sort of a direct relationship between a man and his Creator.

No manager is morally motivated in the making of disciplinary rules. He would like to have all his boys go to heaven when they die—of course he would; but his present concern is the winning of baseball games.

Essentially, I want the whole organization to be known as gentlemen—and I put the emphasis on the "gentle" part. There are no rules for this. Gentlemen adjust themselves to the requirements. If a man does not have gentlemanly instincts, we shall talk to him and help him. Ninety-nine out of one hundred men have instinctively gentlemanly attitudes; but the one can give us much trouble.

No man should be outside the hotel at a late hour, because you are called early, and should be in your room early, and weary, if the boys on the field have done their jobs right. You should have eight hours sleep, so eleven o'clock is late enough, as long as you are called at seven.

I want you to deport yourselves as you would in your own home. I don't want any man to leaven the whole loaf. One man that's obscene or loud, or vulgar, or in any way out of line can give seasoning to the whole mess of pottage, and make everyone seem to be as he is. It is your own business, and you can be your own corrective. We cannot tolerate gross conduct.

PROSPECTS AND SUSPECTS Joe Taylor ♦ A tall, rough, sea-going Negro who allegedly plays a great game when sober. He has a reputation for being a complete rounder—a fence screeching tomcat with not enough females in sight. 'Tis said he even plays a good game with a snoot full. This fellow can run and he can throw and he can hit the ball "a fur piece." I don't know how old he is. So far as I can find out, no one does. My guess is somewhere between 20 and 40. Age doesn't matter because he is fast, agile, and obviously full of confidence. He is presently hitting .325 and 24 doubles and 16 home runs. Taylor bears such a vile reputation that I guess I couldn't have the remotest interest in him, but he impressed me very much as a player. *Taylor was 30 years old when Rickey saw him and filed this report. He played briefly for three major league teams, 1954–59.*

There's no character in history that can compare with Jesus as a man, if nothing more. Yes, I believe in that.

If a man has no moral tone, God help him to get some. You can't make men good by talk. Men have got to elect their fidelities to their fathers and mothers, and wives or anyone else—have to elect it from within, have to superimpose it on yourself, nobody can make you count. If you aren't going to be decent from self-restriction, nobody can make you—just can't be done.

I'm saying I believe in God. Some people don't. I'm a pretty poor disciple of the teachings of my parents and the following of a man of his Holy Father. I'm very humble about that. I'm not moralizing at all; but, if I were, I would not apologize for it.

No man in the world anywhere has a right to expect more from the woman he marries than he has to give to her in cleanliness of mind or body. He's an inferior person who thinks differently, who thinks that a woman should give him more in pureness and devotion, in background and health, than he is able to offer to her. That's the moral side of it.

Imbued as I am with the virtues of connubial bliss, I naturally take pleasure in seeing happily married ballplayers.

You give me 25 men who have a basic, fundamental, religious background, and you don't have much work to do. They will do it from within, out. They will know what they should do and what they shouldn't do. They know the meaning of the words "good health" and "temperance" and "honesty" and "truth"—the whole lot of assets that make character. You don't have to lecture them, or talk to them. If ballplayers—all of them—were like that, you managers would not have very much trouble.

PROSPECTS AND SUSPECTS **Robert Anderson** ♦ I would not be surprised if he is not ignorant of vice, and if so, it is wonderful. (*year unknown*)

The spiritual life cannot go too deep.

◇

The big leagues is a beautiful time in a ballplayer's life. He has every-thing. He has every reason in the world for being happy and useful. But he doesn't appreciate it until he's without it and has lost it—man's extremity* is God's chance. A ballplayer has to think about these things. *Rickey had in mind the end of a player's career and its attendant adversity.

Idleness: The Devil's Playground

What should be done to make sports more moral?

The answer could be a generalization, but I will quickly go from a big answer to a little one. The most dangerous moral hazard in the field of professional sport is leisure. It applies not only to baseball, where men are employed for only four hours out of the twenty-four; it applies to all professional sports.

In the first place, players receive compensations very much above the rate of pay of employees in all other jobs, professional, industrial, or what-not. In the second place, the players are very young men, beginning, say, at eighteen years of age. The average major-league club in baseball will average between twenty-six and twenty-seven years. Minor-league clubs are younger.

The use of sudden surplus funds in the hands of very young men affords another hazard, of course; but this particular hazard only adds to the one I regard as most disturbing—namely, the use of leisure time. "Nothing to do" is the most damnable thing that can come to a youth. I am sure that I have lost two major-league pennants because of rainy days. Every temptation that can come to a boy in the immoral field—women, wine, and gambling—presents itself so easily to idle youngsters. Idleness even more than monotony wrecks the morals of boys and girls more than anything I know. Through the ages, it has been the greatest enemy of adolescents. When one has nothing to do, he is so apt to do the so-called pleasurable thing, the thing closest at hand requiring no thought or industry—and usually indulges in the course of least resistance. Thank heaven, it so frequently takes the direction of nothing more than the movies. But, as boys get older, it can take the form of more personal physical enjoyments.

PROSPECTS AND SUSPECTS **Dave Wickersham** ♦ This chap has had some sort of serious operation on his upper jaw—the roof of his mouth indeed and he is in front of a further operation. His father is a farmer, I would say, a fairly prosperous farmer. He raises 10,000 bushels of apples per year. David pays his own way through school. He waits on tables. He has the only baseball scholarship at Athens. He neither drinks nor smokes, and he has never had a girl. I mean by that, he has never "dated." That might lead some reader of this memorandum to think that David goes in the direction of eunuchry. I don't think that at all. He is simply a country boy who doesn't find his schoolwork too easy, having made "C" plus in his first two years at Ohio University. His mind is on a career in professional baseball. The boy wants to make everything subordinate to a baseball career. *Dave Wickersham pitched for 10 years, 1960–1969, in the major leagues for Kansas City, Detroit and Pittsburgh, compiling a record of 68 victories and 57 defeats.*

I offered millhands, plowboys, high-school kids a better way of life. They rose from sandlots to big-city diamonds. In a month they earned more than they could have earned in a year. And no man who signed a contract with me has ever suffered, educationally or morally. If he chose to remain in school, I helped him. When he quit the Cardinal chain, he had learned the lessons of "clean living" and "moral stamina."

Know about a boy, his parents, where he lives, where he's been and what his interest is. When you ask a boy if he's married and if he has a baby—you'll see an interest there and you may find out he's sending things home or writing pretty regularly—you can tell a lot about a boy that has continuous affection for his home. You don't have to ask many questions about that boy. The family ties hold a man. That's the reason of basic religion. It's a marvelous thing. It holds a man.

CHAPTER NINE

A Man of Many Facets

*R*ickey's words and deeds in his many roles touched the lives of all who came into contact with him. In this section, his contemporaries tell what they remember about the Mahatma.

"Rickey is a man of many facets—all turned on."

—Red Smith

Executive, Manager, and Player

Branch Rickey is a player, manager, executive, lawyer, preacher, horse-trader, spellbinder, innovator, husband and father and grandfather, farmer, logician, obscurantist, reformer, financier, sociologist, crusader, sharper, father confessor, checker-shark, friend and fighter. Judas Priest! What a character!

—*Red Smith*

Mr. Rickey drafted me twice while I was in the minors, first for the Dodgers and then two years later (after 1952 season) for the Pirates. I spent 15 years with the Pirates. I guess he saw something in me he liked." Roy Face led the National League three years in saves and holds the all-time winning percentage for a single season (.947, 18-1 in 1959).

—*Elroy "Roy" Face, Pirate relief specialist*

On the Pirates team (1951) Rickey inherited when he moved to Pittsburgh: We had a lot of triple threat men—slip, fumble, and fall. When Mr. Rickey left the Pirates I used to kid him about him being in the ninth year of a five-year plan. But, I was only kidding because going back to when I was a 15-year-old boy, when I first knew Mr. Rickey, even his "hello" was interesting and challenging. If he ever played "Jeopardy," he would have swept the board.

—*Joe Garagiola (1946–54)*

◇

Despite his lack of success the past two years in Pittsburgh, Branch Rickey still ranks as the smartest baseball man in the business today, if not the smartest of all time. If you don't believe me, just ask the executives, managers, coaches, and players who have played or done business with the Mahatma the past forty years. I have yet to see one cast a dissenting vote.

—*Al Abrams*, Pittsburgh Post-Gazette *(1953)*

Jake Pitler managed the Newport News, a Dodger farm club in the Piedmont League. In 1944, Rickey had assigned 15 boys, 17 years or younger, including outfielder Edwin "Duke" Snider and pitcher Clem Labine, to the Class D club. "When we took off in our bus on a road trip we were loaded with comic books and candy bars," remembers Pitler, "but we carried practically no shaving cream."

There were things in heaven and on earth not dreamed of then in Dizzy's philosophy, things like charge accounts and bank checks, whose existence he discovered after joining the Cardinals. He found that if he signed a check, a man would give him money and later Mr. Rickey would take care of the man. If he bought something and said, "charge it," Mr. Rickey would take care of that.

—Red Smith

Dizzy Dean liked most of all to drop into Rickey's office unannounced, place his huge feet on the boss's desk, lean back and talk country-style. One cold December day he stopped by and then left by the back door as the exhausted Rickey walked into the main room to meet the press, out of character—his jacket off, tie hanging loosely, his collar unbuttoned, his hair rumpled, and a ring of sweat on his forehead. "By Judas Priest!" he began, "By Judas Priest! If there were more like him in baseball, just one, as God is my judge, I'd get out of the game."

Rickey has a private plane and pilot. There isn't a team on the Dodgers farm roster which he does not visit to supervise. He'll fly a couple thousand miles to help decide on the location of a new water cooler or the color of a uniform. When it comes to player deals,

Rickey is unquestionably the manager. Who manages the Dodgers? Shotton during the game. Rickey, 365 days a year!

—*Sports editor Jimmy Powers on Branch Rickey*

By 1925, the St. Louis Cardinals has a solid baseball team, yet had not won a pennant. The problem was the manager, one Branch Rickey. A genius at spotting talent, a brilliant strategist, he could not lead players to victory. Too smart, they said. Talks way over the head of the team. After the 1924 season when the team finished in sixth place, Breadon knew what must be done. He tried to get Rickey to step down, voluntarily and peacefully, but Branch just didn't want to let go. He was evasive and elusive.

In late May 1925, Sam Breadon took a train to Pittsburgh where the Cardinals were wallowing in the cellar of the National League. He summoned Rickey to his hotel room and told him he was through as a manager.

Branch Rickey protested. "You can't do this to me, Sam. You're ruining me."

Sam Breadon shook his head and replied: "I'm doing you the greatest favor one man ever did for another." Branch Rickey was kicked upstairs to the front office where his talents could flower. Rogers Hornsby became the new manager.

You can't beat Mr. Rickey. I'm inclined to side with Bob Carpenter when he said that if Mr. Rickey were elected president and sent to Washington, he would own the government in 30 days.

—*Gus Mancuso, Cincinnati Reds coach*

The quality of Branch Rickey's mind can best be demonstrated by the way he cornered the young talent after the United States got into World War II. Everybody else stopped signing kids. "They'll be going into the army," they said, "and who knows which ones will come back." Rickey signed twice as many. "Some of them will be coming back," he said, "and we'll have them." The next year he was in Brooklyn doing the same thing. In 1946, the first postwar year, Brooklyn and St. Louis, the two teams he had built, battled each other into the first play-off series in baseball history. Unfortunately, his old team beat his new one.

—*Leo Durocher, major-league manager Brooklyn 1939–48,*
New York 1948–55, Chicago 1966–72, Houston 1973

I got a million dollars worth of free advice and a very small raise.

—*Eddie Stanky (1943–53)*

We were coming out of Sandusky, Ohio and had Mr. Rickey's nephew, Rickey Eckert, with us as a passenger.

We had just got airborne when I looked over at the youngster and noticed he was getting sick. As he bent over, I pulled a newspaper away from Mr. Rickey and got it under the nephew just in time to save him from messing up the floor. When it was all over, I tossed the paper out the window.

The boss asked the boy if he was feeling all right, and after being assured that the sickness was over, Mr. Rickey turned to me and asked: "Was that the sports page?"

—*Moose Redhead, Branch Rickey's private pilot*

Right after I graduated from high school (1953) my coach took me to a tryout at Forbes Field in Pittsburgh. Mr. Rickey and Rex Bowen (scout) stood behind the batting cage and watched me hit. I hit some over the fence and a couple off the scoreboard. Mr. Rickey told Rex Bowen to get a contract for me, and to sign me up. When I went to Bowen's office I met and fell in love with his secretary. That young lady has been my wife for many years. So, I guess Mr. Rickey is responsible for my wife and I meeting and getting married!

Mr. Rickey also came to scout me at a game in Portland, Oregon while I was playing for the Pirates' Hollywood, California club. I had a good day with the bat and based on Mr. Rickey's recommendation I was called up to the big leagues three days later. I guess I owe Mr. Rickey quite a debt of gratitude for his confidence in me, but I was so young and Mr. Rickey was so famous for knowing so much about everything that I was always afraid to talk to him. I guess you could say that Mr. Rickey even managed to touch the lives of people who never had much contact with him.

—*Bill Mazeroski, former Pirate great (1956–72)*

As a college coach Rickey demanded of his Michigan University players a sense of "adventure," of daring-do on the bases, of constantly attacking their opponents' weaknesses. In one game in which his Wolverines were comfortably leading, he signaled his slow-footed catcher Russ Baer to steal second simply to underscore his point. "Branch gave me the signal to steal," said Baer, "all the players on our bench stood up and cheered me as I lumbered my way to second base, where I was tagged out by ten feet." When he picked himself up and dusted off the dirt, Baer returned to the Wolverine bench, his teammates still applauding and his coach sporting a huge grin. "Adventure, Russell, adventure," he shouted.

Always concerned with economy, Rickey instructed his Dodger scouts to be brief in their reports to him. One day he wired a scout to ask if a certain player was ready to be promoted. The answer, in a telegram delivered at his office, contained one word: "Yes."

"Yes, what?" Rickey fired back.

"Yes, sir," the scout replied.

Catching and playing outfield for the New York Highlanders in 1907 Rickey batted .182. He finished last in the league in fielding percentage for catchers and outfielders. In one eleven game stretch he committed nine errors. On June 28, 1907 he allowed thirteen stolen bases, a record for a nine-inning game. The Highlanders released him at the season's end.

Sharper, Horse-Trader, and Checker-Shark

Branch Rickey traded Dizzy Dean to the Cubs in 1938. The comparative statistics: Dean's record prior to trade, 134-75, .640 PCT over seven years, including 37 wins over 1936–37; after the trade, 16-8, .667, over five years. Rickey's Cardinals received $185,000 cash and three players: pitcher Curt Davis, 40-28, .590 PCT, over two-and-one-half seasons; pitcher Clyde Shoun, 25-23, .520 PCT, over four seasons. Rickey sent utility outfielder Tuck Stainback to the Phillies for the prevailing waiver price.

When Rickey was president/general manager of the Cardinals (1917–18, 1925–42), the General Foods people wanted to sign Jerome Hanna (Dizzy) Dean to an exclusive, year-round contract as a champion of breakfast food. There was to be a conference about money and Diz asked Mr. Rickey to help with negotiations. Branch agreed willingly.

"Now Jerome," said Mr. Rickey in his fatherly way, "when we begin talking money let me handle them. I know how to deal with these people so you just sit there. Don't make a move. Don't say anything. I'll do the talking."

"I gotcha, Mr. Rickey," said Diz.

The meeting was held in a suite in the Hotel Coronado, just a few blocks from the heart of downtown St. Louis.

"I understand, gentlemen, that you are offering Mr. Dean $18,000 to become your representative. Is that correct?" Mr. Rickey asked. The men from General Foods nodded in agreement. "It would seem to me," Mr. Rickey continued, "that a company as large and prosperous as General Foods could spare $2,000 more and make it an even $20,000. After all, Mr. Dean is an illustrious man."

There were reasons, it developed, that General Foods didn't want to pay $20,000 for Mr. Dean's services. The budget called for $18,000 and that was as high as they were going. "In that case," said Mr. Rickey, "I think I can suggest an alternative. I note that the contract has several clauses, one of which gives you Mr. Dean on an exclusive basis. If you'll strike out the 'exclusive' clause, we'll sign for $12,000." Before the men from General Foods could reply, Dizzy jumped from his chair. "Wait a minute, Mr. Rickey," he said, "You're going in the wrong direction. They already offered $18,000. How come you'll settle for $12,000?"

Mr. Rickey looked at Diz as a father does a wayward child. Then he closed his brief case, donned his hat and coat, and left the room. The contract was signed for $18,000. To his grave, Mr. Rickey swore that he would have gotten $20,000 if Jerome hadn't broken up his game.

Once, Rickey locked himself and Syracuse club owner Ed Landgraf in a hotel room while they negotiated the purchase of Sunny Jim Bottomly's contract. After several hours they emerged, all smiles for the cameras. Rickey announced that Bottomly was a Cardinal. The press asked how this was accomplished. "By persuasion," was Rickey's cryptic reply. To another reporter in St Louis who asked how he pulled it off, Rickey answered, "By logic." Later, to a third reporter, he explained, "By appealing to his sense of integrity." Finally, years later, the same query and probably the most truthful answer, "By more money."

"There's only one way to get the best of that Rickey. You let him talk for three hours on the strong and weak points of the players he wants to scoop. Then, when Branch says, 'Is it a deal?' you snap, 'No,' and walk out on him."

—Casey Stengel, major-league manager, Brooklyn 1934–36,
Boston 1938–43, New York Yankees 1949–60,
New York Mets 1962–65

◇

Mr. Rickey had more knowledge of baseball than anyone else and he knew his ballplayers, but when you talked money to him you could get none of it. He was always going to the vault to give you a nickel's change.

—Enos Slaughter (1938–59)

◇

Mr. Rickey had a heart of gold, and he kept it.

—Gene Hermanski (1943–53)

◇

In 1949, when the Brooklyn Dodgers were in a pennant race with the St. Louis Cardinals, Branch Rickey approached the Pittsburgh Pirates in search of pitching help. Bill Werle, a lefthander, was one of the best pitchers the seventh-place Pirates had. The financially strapped Pirates needed all the help they could get. Rickey proposed a deal to Roy Hamey, the Pirates' general manager. "I'll give you $250,000 for Bill Werle," he said.

Hamey said he'd take the money, only to have Rickey explain that he didn't mean $250,000 in cash. He would trade five Brooklyn "farmhands"—each, in Rickey's estimation, worth $50,000.

The deal never went through. But that was the way Rickey dealt. He put his own price tags on players.

Mr. Rickey was the forerunner of the management side that brought about the players' union organization. With his parsimonious attitude to the baseball player, he did more than any other person to bring about the union.

—*Ralph Kiner (1946–55)*

◇

Mr. Rickey went out of his way to do so much to put blacks in the major leagues. He could tell you so many things, Mr. Rickey, just like my mother or father reading a book to me as a youngster. He made me a better catcher, a better person on and off the field. He made me a completely changed individual.

—*Roy Campanella (1948–57)*

◇

Mr. Rickey was a very smart baseball man and was a great speaker on most any subject. He was also a very tough negotiator at contract time. When he was trying to get you to sign a contract he always said that your earned run average (ERA) was too high. The next year your ERA would be down, but Mr. Rickey said that you didn't win enough games. And so on it went year after year.

—*Max Lanier (1938–53)*

◇

Mr. Rickey had great insight into everyday life as well as baseball. In one of our player meetings he once said, "Never play checkers with a man who carries his own board." I never forgot it.

—*Bob Purkey (1954–66), former Pirate pitcher*

Preacher and Spellbinder

As a student of technique, he was simply unchallenged. Our first training camp was at Sanford, Florida, and for one hour every morning Mr. Rickey would lecture on baseball fundamentals. How to field each position, the correct techniques for fingering a baseball and throwing it, for getting a lead off base, sliding. What it took to be a great hitter. Every phase of the game. On the second morning I hired a male stenographer, sat him down and told him not to miss a word. Other people gave instruction. Mr. Rickey knew.

—*Leo Durocher*

◇

I would send and receive notes via a bellboy. I was afraid being in the same room with Mr. Rickey would mesmerize me.

—*Bill Veeck, owner: Browns, Indians, White Sox*

◇

By the time Mr. Rickey got through with you, you were sure that you were the luckiest guy in the world to receive and sign the contract he offered you. Besides, you always felt you had been uplifted, just listening to him talk.

—*Terry Moore (1935–48)*

◇

He was a great believer in players being family men. At this contract session, he talked of the joys of marriage. I agreed with him. I was married and said I thought it was fine, too. He told me a ballplayer should put money aside and prepare for the future. I agreed with him again, told him that was what I had in mind and if he'd give me the money I wanted, I would follow his advice. I just kept agreeing with him and I finally got exactly what I wanted.

—*Marty Marion (1940–53)*

It varied with me. One time he'd listen while I talked. Sometimes he never let me talk at all. He'd always be sympathetic but then he would start talking real big, and before he was through I'd be reaching for the pen. I didn't know what he was talking about half the time, but it sure sounded beautiful.

—*Enos Slaughter*

Framed and hung in Rickey's offices in St. Louis, Brooklyn, and Pittsburgh:

He that will not reason is a bigot
He that cannot reason is a fool
He that dares not reason is a slave

A hypocritical preacher.

—*Judge Kenesaw Mountain Landis, baseball commissioner, 1920–44*

Branch Rickey was a friend of mine and I admired him. Branch Rickey was a credit to baseball, and to Christianity. He was a man of deep piety and integrity—that rare combination of a "man's man" and a Christian man, at the same time.

—*Reverend Billy Graham, March 18, 1967*

When Rickey makes up his mind, he'll walk through a 10-foot brick wall.

—*Larry MacPhail, general manager,*
president: Reds, Dodgers, Yankees

Branch Rickey was a multi-talented man, as exciting and spellbinding as anybody I've ever known.

—*Joe Garagiola*

◊

[Mr. Rickey] was a stickler for details, from the way the players dressed on the field to how the hot dogs were served. He liked to remind the players, "you reap what you sow."

—*George Kissell, senior field coordinator, St. Louis Cardinals*

Innovator

One of Mr. Rickey's strategy theories was the five-man infield, in which he'd bring in either the left fielder or right fielder to play about 10 to 15 feet from the batter, either on the first or third base line. The idea was that the close positioning of the outfielder would be able to foil the bunt attempt. One day during spring training practice he sent me to the plate. When the pitch came, the outfielder (on the third base line) and first baseman were so close they were practically down my throat. Instead of bunting, I swung away to cross them up. I hit a whistling line drive right at the head of the charging first baseman, who spun away and fell down in avoiding getting beaned.

Mr. Rickey charged the plate and grabbed the bat from me, "No more, no more. You're too good a hitter to try this play."

When we resumed, he brought in Cal Abrams, a left fielder who is Jewish. When Abrams assumed his position along the third base line, he wisecracked, "I don't see you bringing in any Christians to play this position."

—*Ralph Branca, Dodger pitcher (1944–56)*

Mr. Rickey once told the story about how he hired Allen Roth, the statistician in 1947.

Roth came down from his native Canada where he had been doing statistics for hockey teams. He wanted to sell Mr. Rickey on doing statistics for the Brooklyn Dodgers. In those days no one did statistics like they do nowadays.

Roth met Mr. Rickey in his office in Brooklyn and proceeded to show him figures why Duke Snider would hit better against certain pitchers and why Pee Wee Reese would play better on weekends than on Mondays or Tuesdays. All kinds of weird statistics that no one had ever heard of before.

Mr. Rickey listened to all this.

"Mr. Roth," he finally answered. "That's like telling me how many nudges of the nose it would take someone to push a peanut up Pike's Peak. Who cares!"

But about two weeks later, Mr. Rickey realized what value Roth's statistics were and he brought him back to Brooklyn and hired him. Roth stayed with the Dodgers all through their Brooklyn days and moved to the West Coast with them when they shifted the franchise to Los Angeles. Branch Rickey was the first man in baseball to hire a statistician.

Rickey is one of baseball's immortals. As long as the game lives, so will the memory of Branch Rickey and the contributions he made to it.

—*Gussie Busch, Jr.,* Globe Democrat, *December 11, 1965*

I believe you have done more than any other American in breaking down "race hatred." I hope you will forgive me when I say it is terrible that you have to grow old. I wonder if you can be replaced.

—*Art Rooney, owner of the Pittsburgh Steelers,*
in a letter to Mr. Rickey (2/13/52)

In Memoriam: December, 1965

Almost everybody who knew Rickey respected him. They admired him and, up to a point, revered him. There were some who disliked Branch Rickey intensely. In his long career in baseball, one that was often misunderstood and not always appreciated, every conceivable epithet was directed at him. But he was never swayed from the course he believed he had to follow. He was the greatest man baseball has ever known.

—*Bob Burnes*, St. Louis Globe-Democrat

Only Alexander Cartright, the man who drew up the original baseball rules in 1845 and who had the inspiration of placing the bases 90 feet apart, had a greater impact on baseball than Branch Rickey. Rickey was a genius, a man who could have attained the top rank in any business or profession. Baseball is fortunate that this extraordinary person chose to channel his talents in its direction. So dominating a figure was Rickey that he altered the course of its history.

—*Arthur Daley, writing in* The New York Times

Rickey had style, and he was unafraid. He was the greatest man in baseball. There was a lot of hustler in him and plenty of actor. But he came on strongest as an evangelist. Smaller men ridiculed him, claiming that he was a phony; but their envy caused them to exaggerate Rickey's defects. He was a guy who played the angles. There has never been anyone like him in organized sport—I doubt that there ever will be again.

—*Jimmy Cannon*, New York Journal-American

Only the naïve would believe that all Rickey was trying to do was break baseball's color barrier. B.R. slyly had Jackie Robinson hand-picked, and he had Roy Campanella and Don Newcombe thoroughly scouted before deciding, in 1945, that his Christian conscience would no longer permit him to discriminate against his black brother. No matter how cynically or sincerely the Mahatma's motives might be evaluated, he will be remembered by the Negro for having opened up a new vista for the race.

—*Bob Broeg*, St. Louis Post-Dispatch

What Rickey did, he did with a flourish. People liked him immensely, looking upon him with awe and reverence, or they couldn't stand him. He was the most potent front-office man in the history of baseball. He will long be remembered as the man who started the farm system, who opened the doors of baseball to the Negro, as the man who forced expansion. Rickey could talk on almost any subject. He had a brilliant command of the English language. He could captivate an audience of three or a crowd of a thousand. True, he sometimes wore his halo too loose; but he was a legend in his time. It's doubtful that we will see the likes of Branch Rickey again.

—*Lester Biederman*, Pittsburgh Press

"Baseball is a game for boys," Rickey once declared as he scanned the future. "Football will never replace baseball as our national game." The dangers to baseball, he said, lie at the professional level. Rickey defined baseball's problems as, one, equalization of teams, particularly in the American League; and, two, expansion to new population centers.

—*Watson Spoelstra*, Detroit News

When Mr. Rickey spoke, the angels listened. At the age of 82, he could come to Chicago, agree to speak briefly, then spellbind people for more than an hour. Branch Rickey did many things in baseball—some that we liked and some we didn't. He could build championship clubs; no one can fault him on that score. The fact that Rickey used slave labor—the farm teams—to insure the success of those clubs was something few could appreciate. But no one will ever forget one thing that Branch Rickey did: He was the first to give the colored man his rightful place in baseball.

—*David Condon*, Chicago Tribune

I will always defend Mr. Rickey. I owe him a debt of gratitude. I will always speak out with the utmost praise for the man.

—*Jackie Robinson*

Very probably he was the greatest man ever to devote his life to a game, any game. Two strains come through from the life of Branch Rickey. One was his idealism; the other was his pragmatism. "He wouldn't take a drink," Casey Stengel once said, "but he'd hire a man who would if he could slide across home place." The words "genius" and "great" are thrown around loosely; but Branch Rickey was the real thing. He was a genius because, in a highly competitive milieu, he was 360 feet ahead of everybody. He was great because he had the courage of his convictions—or, more accurately, his innovations. Rickey made his first mark on baseball with the farm system; but he did other things. For example, he led the battle for the Continental League, which spurred expansion. He introduced mechanical aids to improve playing skills. But his greatest monument to baseball was the breaking of the color barrier.

—*Larry Merchant*, Philadelphia Daily News

He was not only a topflight executive, but the greatest revolutionary the game has ever known. No one has ever approached Rickey's talents for building baseball dynasties on a shoestring. His appearance, his manner, his oratory, all about him there was sort of a Churchillian style. As a builder of empires, Rickey was supreme. As a trader of talent, he was a genius. Branch Rickey was probably the most glamorous name in all baseball history.

—*Lou Smith*, Cincinnati Enquirer

Phil Pepe, veteran sports reporter, was the first to inform Jackie Robinson of Branch Rickey's death. Pepe was working for the New York World-Telegram & Sun, an evening paper, when news of Mr. Rickey's death came across the wire. Pepe called Robinson to inform him and get his reaction. Upon hearing the news, Robinson did not reply. After a silent pause (that seemed like an eternity to Pepe, but in reality was only four or five seconds) Robinson spoke, not to Pepe, but to his wife, Rachel, "Rae, take this call . . . Mr. Rickey just died." Jackie then collected himself and after a few minutes came back on the line to comment.

Branch Rickey

Branch Rickey, major league baseball's one and only Renaissance man, influenced baseball more deeply than anyone else. He built the farm club system of producing major league players, pioneered the application of technology in instruction, and opened the way for blacks and Latinos to play in the major leagues.

Rickey was born in Pike County Ohio, December 20, 1881.

He received a Bachelor of Arts degree at Ohio Wesleyan University (Delaware, Ohio), a Doctor of Jurisprudence degree from the University of Michigan, and held honorary degrees from Ohio Wesleyan, McKendree College and the University of Rochester.

He married Jane Moulton of Lucasville, Ohio in 1906. He and Jane had six children—five daughters and a son, Branch Jr., who was associated with the Brooklyn club as his father's assistant.

As a major league baseball player he caught for the Cincinnati Reds (1905), the St. Louis Browns (1906), and the New York Highlanders (1907). He later managed both St. Louis teams and also served as general manager of the Browns, Cardinals, Brooklyn Dodgers and Pittsburgh Pirates.

A veteran of World War I, Rickey served in France as a major in the chemical warfare division. He had a lifelong interest in the development of youth. Rickey organized the Knot Hole Gang to combat juvenile delinquency and develop future fans for baseball, and throughout his career he was associated with the YMCA.

Twice cited by *The Sporting News* as baseball's executive of the year, Rickey in his lengthy career at various times was a school teacher, a lawyer, a college star in baseball and football, a college coach and athletic director, then a professional competitor in both sports, a baseball manager in both leagues, an administrator in both pro football and baseball, and an owner in pro baseball.

Rickey passed away on December 9, 1965.

Timeline

1881   Born December 20 in Lucasville, Ohio

1898   Takes job as country schoolteacher

1901   Enrolls at Ohio Wesleyan University (OWU)

1903   Becomes baseball coach at OWU (Thomas racial incident provides an early preview of Rickey's attitude toward race in baseball)

1904   Graduates from OWU

1904   Signs pro baseball contract with Cincinnati Reds (dismissed for refusing to play on Sundays; traded to ChiSox)

1904   Becomes coach (football) at Allegheny College

1905   Signs at catcher for St. Louis Browns (parents sick—returns home)

1906   Marries Jane Moulton on June 1—plays with Browns again

1906   Hired as football, basketball and baseball coach at OWU

1907   Enters Law School/Coaches at University of Michigan (until 1911)

1907   Plays catcher for New York Highlanders (gives up record 13 stolen bases in one game)

1909   Stricken with tuberculosis (Rickey spent his convalescent period in a sanitarium, as was the custom at that time)

1910   Hired as head baseball coach at the University of Michigan

1911   Graduates from Michigan University Law School

1912   Hired as an executive by the St. Louis Browns

1913   Becomes Browns' field manager

1916   Becomes head of Browns' front office

1917   Hired as president by the St. Louis Cardinals

1918   Enlists in July in Chemical Warfare Unit of U.S. Army; commissioned as major and assigned to duty station in France

1918   Released in December from active duty

1919   Becomes field manager of St. Louis Cardinals (as well as president)

1921   National Agreement is signed (allowing major league ownership of minor league clubs); Rickey begins building Cardinals "farm system"

1925   Begins his first "tryout" camp at Danville, Illinois

1925   Fired as Cardinal manager and named vice president

1926   Cardinals win pennant and defeat Yankees in the World Series

1926   Trades Rogers Hornsby for Frankie Frisch and cash

1927   Cardinals finish in 2nd place

1928   Cardinals win the NL pennant, but lose Series to Yankees

1930   Cardinals win the NL pennant, but lose Series to Athletics

1930   Signs Dizzy Dean

1931   Cardinals win NL pennant and World Series (4-3 over Athletics)

1934   Rickey's Gashouse Gang wins World Series

1938   Judge Landis attacks Rickey's farm system in "Cedar Rapids Case," eventually 74 Cardinal farm hands (including Pete Reiser) are declared free agents by Landis

1938   Trades Dizzy Dean to Cubs

1938   Signs Stan Musial

1940   Trades Joe "Ducky" Medwick to Dodgers

1942   Cardinals win World Series over Yankees

1942   Resigns from Cardinals and is hired by Brooklyn Dodgers as president

1943   With approval of Dodgers board of directors Rickey begins search for "the right man" to break the color line

1945   On August 18 meets with Robinson for the first time and reveals plan to him

1946   Signs Jackie Robinson to minor league (Montreal) contract

1946   Dodgers lose the NL pennant in a playoff to Cardinals (both teams developed by Rickey)

1947   On April 10, Dodgers sign Jackie Robinson
1947   Wins first pennant with Brooklyn; Dodgers lose to Yankees
       in the World Series
1947   Jackie Robinson named Rookie of the Year
1948   Ventures into professional football (football Dodgers), which
       later fails
1949   Dodgers win the NL pennant but are again defeated by the
       Yankees in the World Series
1949   Jackie Robinson wins the NL Most Valuable Player Award
1950   Resigns as Brooklyn Dodger president after being forced out
       by Walter O'Malley
1950   Signs with Pittsburgh Pirates as vice president of operations
1953   Trades Pirate slugger Ralph Kiner to Cubs
1955   Resigns Pirate position—becomes chairman of the board at
       Pittsburgh
1959   Resigns as CEO at Pittsburgh
1959   Becomes president of the proposed Continental League
       (New York, Buffalo, Toronto, Minneapolis/St. Paul,
       Houston, Dallas/Ft. Worth, Atlanta, Denver)
1960   Pirates (bearing an obvious Rickey "stamp") win the World
       Series
1961   Only son, Branch Rickey, Jr., dies of hepatitis
1962   Attends Jackie Robinson's induction into The Hall of Fame
1962   Responding to pressure from Rickey and the Continental
       League, NL and AL expand (NL adds New York Mets and
       Houston Astros; AL adds Los Angeles Angels and allows the
       Washington franchise to relocate to Minneapolis)
1963   Hired by the St. Louis Cardinals as consultant
1964   Cardinals win first World Series since 1946
1964   His documentary book, The American Diamond is published
1965   Fired by Cardinals
1965   Dies on December 9
1967   Elected into The National Baseball Hall of Fame

Branch Rickey's Playing and Managing Records

Rickey, Wesley Branch (The Mahatma)

Bats Left, Throws Right
5'9" 175 lbs.

b. Dec. 20, 1881, Lucasville, Ohio, d. Dec. 9, 1965,
Columbia, Missouri
Manager 1913–15, 1919–25, Hall of Fame 1967

BRANCH RICKEY'S PLAYING RECORD

		G	AB	H	2B	3B	HR	HR%	R	RBI	BB	SO	SB	BA	SA	Pinchhit AB	Pinchhit H	G by Position
1905 STL	A	1	3	0	0	0	0	0.0	0	0	0		0	.000	.000	0	0	C-1
1906		64	201	57	7	3	3	1.5	22	24	16		4	.284	.393	7	2	C-54, OF-1
1907 NY	A	54	137	25	2	3	0	0.0	16	15	11		4	.182	.241	12	1	OF-22, C-11, 1B-9
1914 STL	A	2	2	0	0	0	0	0.0	0	0	0	1	0	.000	.000	2	0	
4 yrs.		119	343	82	9	6	3	0.9	38	39	27	1	8	.239	.327	21	3	C-66, OF-23, 1B-9

BRANCH RICKEY'S MANAGING RECORD

		G	W	L	%	Standing	
1913 STL	A	12	5	6	.455	8	8
1914		159	71	82	.464	5	
1915		159	63	91	.409	6	
1919 STL	N	138	54	83	.394	7	
1920		155	75	79	.487	5	
1921		154	87	66	.569	3	
1922		154	85	69	.552	3	
1923		154	79	74	.516	5	
1924		154	65	89	.422	6	
1925		38	13	25	.342	8	4
10 yrs.		1277	597	664	.473		

Bibliography

Books
Frommer, Harvey. *Rickey and Robinson*. New York: Macmillan, 1982.

Hood, Robert E. *The Gashouse Gang*. New York: William Morrow, 1976.

Mann, Arthur. *Branch Rickey: American in Action*. Boston: Houghton Mifflin, 1957.

Polner, Murray. *Branch Rickey*. New York: Atheneum, 1982.

Rickey, Branch, with Robert Riger. *The American Diamond*. New York: Simon & Schuster, 1965.

Tygiel, Jules. *Baseball's Great Experiment: Jackie Robinson and His Legacy*. New York: Oxford University Press, 1983.

Wolff, Rick, ed. *The Baseball Encyclopedia*, ninth edition. New York: Macmillan, 1993.

Unpublished Works
Mann, Arthur William, "The Papers of Arthur William Mann," The Collection of the Manuscript Division, Library of Congress, 1970.

Rickey, Wesley Branch, "The Papers of Wesley Branch Rickey," The Collection of the Manuscript Division, Library of Congress, 1972–80.

Acknowledgments

I would like to thank all the persons who helped make this book possible, including:

- Mrs. Mary Eckler—daughter of Mr. Rickey, who encouraged us and kindly gave us permission to publish Rickey's writings.
- Mr. Branch Rickey, grandson of the Mahatma and president of the American Association.
- Jeanine Bucek, sports editor at Macmillan books, for her support, guidance and enthusiasm.
- David Berman—a deep-thinking Texan whose appreciation for the poetics of Rickey's scouting reports sparked the conception of this book.
- Jeffrey M. Flannery—The Manuscript Reference Librarian at the Library of Congress whose enthusiasm and expert assistance guided us through the reams of Rickey's papers.
- The Major League Baseball Alumni Association, for helping us to contact all the old baseball greats.
- Stan Musial, for his insightful retrospective and preface.
- All the former players and associates of Mr. Rickey who responded to our request for personal anecdotes.
- Veteran sports writers Bob Broeg, Jack Lang, and Jack Clary, for reporting and interviewing Mr. Rickey's contemporaries.
- Steve Gietschier of *The Sporting News* in St. Louis, for helping to discover Mr. Rickey's pearls of wisdom and wit.
- Rose Nero, for her support, Josephine and Andrew Monteleone, my dad, for passing along his love of baseball to me.
- And all the word-crunchers in the trenches at Mountain Lion, Inc., the book developer that produced this book: Roy Grisham, Lee Lowenfish, Steve Mann, Joan Mohan, Andrew J. Monteleone, Steve Stovall, Margaret Trejo, and Randy Voorhees.

—John J. Monteleone

Index